The Age of Surge is a must-read for any business leader who aspires to lead their company in the emerging age of exponential innovation. The authors . . . provide a revolutionary framework for . . . digital transformation, by connecting the dots of personal ethos, leadership mindset, organizational systems, company culture, and digital technologies.

—**George Zarkadakis, Digital Lead, Willis Towers Watson;**
Author of *In Our Own Image: Savior or Destroyer?*
The History and Future of Artificial Intelligence

The Age of Surge is transformational innovation in a bottle for leaders and companies seeking to win in the new tech-fueled digital economy!

—**John Schanz, Former Chief Network Officer, Comcast Cable**

The authors begin this book with "start where you are and follow yes." If you're looking to implement OKRs at scale, I say "start where you are and get this book."

—**Ben Lamorte, Co-author of *Objectives and Key Results: Driving***
***Focus, Alignment, and Engagement with OKRs*; Founder of OKRs.com**

We're in an era where emerging companies are disrupting every industry and incumbents in those industries are searching for ways to transform themselves in the face of this competition. *The Age of Surge* provides business leaders with a clear approach to driving and managing the change necessary to truly transform their organizations . . .

—**Sinclair Schuller, Founder and CEO of Apprenda**

The hallmark of the modern enterprise is that every company is a software company. *The Age of Surge* presents fresh and clear thinking on how to manage the ongoing waves of technologies that shape and reshape businesses.

—**Luke Hohman, Founder and CEO, Conteneo;**
Former Board Member, The Agile Alliance

In *The Age of Surge*, Murphy and Mase show they are the dinosaur whisperers, trustworthy and brilliant guides for taking large companies threatened with extinction on a journey to perpetual adaptation and innovation . . . . The Coverage of OKRs 2.0 alone makes the read worthwhile.

—Jay Stanton, Founder and Managing Partner of Jabbok River Group; Faculty at Northwestern McCormick School of Engineering

. . . . *The Age of Surge* shows how to deal with the volatility, uncertainty, complexity, and ambiguity (VUCA) of the world of business. . . . If you're a leader faced with the challenge of pulling an organization into the 21st century, this book is sure to help.

—Jurgen Appelo, Author of *Managing for Happiness*; CEO of Agility Scales

. . . Business leaders of iconic, large corporations and dynamic, young startups alike can benefit from learning more about . . . . the importance of personal and organizational transformation alongside technology to fully experience digital transformation.

—Steve Robinson, General Manager, Client Technical Engagement - IBM Cloud

. . . . With the right digital leadership that promotes creativity, autonomy and speed, executives will soon realize the full potential of the organization to embrace creative destruction and creative regeneration. *The Age of Surge* can be your navigational chart in these disruptive times.

—Victor Fetter, Chief Digital Officer, Vertiv

While most authors of books on digital transformation focus on technology, Murphy and Mase center their discussion on the organizational side of digital. They thoughtfully explore essential topics including leadership, talent management, and communication—important enablers of digital transformation . . .

—Jason Bloomber, President, Intellyx

THE AGE OF
SURGE

THE AGE OF SURGE

A Human-Centered Framework for
Scaling Company-Wide Agility and
Navigating the Digital Tsunami

Brad Murphy & Dr. Carol Mase

Reinvent Press

THE AGE OF SURGE
By Brad Murphy and Dr. Carol Mase

BULK ORDERS AND SPECIAL SALES
Additional books are available at special discounts for bulk purchases for business, sales promotions, or educational use. Special editions, including personalized covers, excerpts of the book, and corporate imprints, can be created in large quantities for special needs. For more information, write to Special Needs at: specialneeds@reinventpress.com

Manuscript Coach: Stacy Ennis   Developmental Editor: Nicholas Valdez
Copyeditor: Jim Forsha   Indexer: Mikael Hornqvist
Interior Designer: Sarah Pierson   Illustrator: Caleb Brown

January 2018:   First Edition

PUBLISHED BY

 Reinvent
Press

7800 Falls of Neuse Rd, Suite 97663
Raleigh, NC 27624
www.reinventpress.com

ISBN-13: 978-0-9996444-1-6 (hardback)
ISBN-13: 978-0-9996444-0-9 (paperback)
ISBN-13: 978-0-9996444-2-3 (ebook)

To my adult children Ashley and Brad, who are now early in their careers and
beginning to appreciate why Dad is so passionate about organizational transformation.
To my wife Julie, who, despite enduring long stretches of neglect (as I obsessed over
helping clients), has remained both my best friend and enduring partner in life.

—*Brad*

To my mentors: George Edwin (engineer),
Richard (physicist), and Michael (endocrinologist)

—*Carol*

~ TABLE OF CONTENTS ~

THE AGE OF
SURGE

ACKNOWLEDGMENTS

Like most, this book stands on the shoulders of other people, many of whom we don't even know. Authors, mentors, colleagues, and clients have all shaped our point of view. Perhaps most significantly, the work we do with our clients provides us with the petri dish of experimentation and learning. For that reason, we want to acknowledge the companies and leaders with whom we work daily. Their courage and tenacity as they face the digital tsunami that heads their way is inspirational.

As first time authors, we knew we needed help in successfully writing a book that would have real potential to help others. We want to especially thank two people in particular who were instrumental: Stacey Ennis helped us take nearly 80 years of combined insights and experience and turn that into an early manuscript. Nick Valdez joined our team as a developmental editor and helped us tease out the wheat from the chaff, and, in the process, transform the early manuscript into a book worthy of publishing.

Lastly, to those who reviewed our early manuscript: Your candid feedback and suggestions transformed the book for us, and now for our readers.

"The complexity of demands upon collective human systems [companies] have recently become larger than an individual human being [can manage]. Once this is true, hierarchical mechanisms are no longer able to impose the necessary coordination of individual behaviors. Instead, interactions characteristic of networks are necessary."

— Yaneer Bar-Yam, *Complexity Rising*

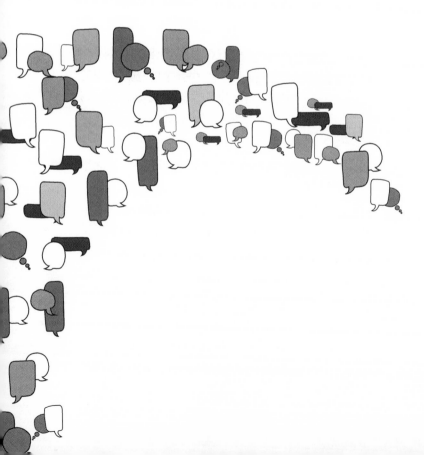

INTRODUCTION

THE DIGITAL TSUNAMI

S teve Chen, Chad Hurley, and Jawed Karim met as early employees of PayPal. Chen and Hurley left in 2002 when eBay acquired the company. They were reunited in 2005 at a party, which they recorded digitally. Intending to share the videos with guests and friends, they confronted the problem of the files being too large to upload. This led them to create a website that would allow people to upload videos they wanted to share — privately or publicly.

Within a year their quest to solve their problem created the tenth most popular site on the Internet: YouTube. By 2006, when Google acquired YouTube, it had become a means for artistic expression; a vehicle to deliver academic courses, lectures, and TED Talks; a standard way to share life with family and friends; and by 2017 had grown to over 1 billion minutes in video watched per day.

The histories of this and other digital powerhouses — such as Netflix, Spotify, Google, Facebook, and Airbnb — have the same motif:

Digital creates novel ways for people to solve problems that matter to them and simultaneously create value for others. In aggregate, enterprises such as these have produced the "Digital Tsunami," a tremendous force that has entirely flooded market ecosystems and forever altered their composition and structure.

In the wake of this digital tsunami, behemoths built on analog must now shift to digital, using both technical and adaptive methods to disrupt themselves. At the same time, leaders of large enterprises find themselves in conditions that are now beyond their control. The solutions they've developed in the past to tackle major technical and organizational problems are no longer useful; worse, they are no longer even functional.

In response to the uncertain digital environment—an environment in which the next major breakthrough is anyone's guess—companies are experimenting with agile and cloud technologies and deploying scaling frameworks to unite business with technology. They are trying to calculate market adjustments, attempting to discover the unknown, striving to harness the unknowable.

Many executives hope to find a roadmap, one that will show them the clearest path through the new terrain of the digital marketplace. They imagine that the terrain can be made solid and predictable. They want to believe they can navigate the marketplace of today like they did the marketplace of yesterday.

The truth is that there is no roadmap for what's coming . . . for no roadmap exists where there are no roads!

Instead, today's businesses find themselves surrounded by waves of change, fluid and unpredictable. One after another, digital waves rise, crest, and fall, breaking away the concrete solutions of the past.

This is the paradigm shift industrial-age corporations need to understand if they want to catch up and participate in the emerging digital market ecosystems. They must become familiar with the problems all are struggling to solve and invent something, *using digital means,* to address them. This new style of business development must work just as well inside the company as it does out in the marketplace.

So how can enterprises navigate and move intentionally across the digital waves? *Surge* explores this very question.

ADAPTIVE ORGANIZATIONS SURGE

What do Netflix, Spotify, and Google all have in common? They represent a new breed of company we now call exponential organizations. By *exponential* we mean companies learning, innovating, and continuously adapting 10 times better, faster, and cheaper than traditional companies.[1]

These exponential organizations (ExOs) are based on transparency, abundance, and autonomy. Moreover, they use digital technology to innovate, disrupt, and grow in radical and dynamic ways. They *surge* ahead of traditional companies.

At the same time, traditional companies are anything but asleep at the wheel. Today, large firms work tirelessly to keep up, pursuing continuous improvements to their business and digital operations. Entire cottage industries of thinkers, consultants, and method junkies promote the benefits of digital as the means for large firms to regain their start-up mojo, often recommending that they master a new more agile or lean process. In fact, you can't escape a daily headline on corporate transformation efforts without enduring the promises and proclaimed advances through scaling agile, DevOps, and lean frameworks—all professing the ability to accelerate organizational agility, innovation, and digital transformation.

Still, in reality, these transformational efforts are bogged down by

---

1   Salim Ismail, *Exponential Organizations: Why New Organizations Are Ten Times Better, Faster, and Cheaper than Yours (and What to Do about It),* with Michael S. Malone and Yuri van Geest (New York: Diversion Books, 2014).

two dangerous, inescapable truths. First, the new and improved work methods of agile and lean are still constrained by traditional management practices, organizational structures, and ingrained cultures—all of which are hostile to the ideas of experimentation and failure. Meanwhile, ExOs thrive on experimentation and learn from failure.

Unlike ExOs, traditional approaches to management are anchored in a worldview that assumes market changes occur over moderate periods and in a linear, stepwise fashion. This conventional view remains committed to seeing competition as the main activity of markets and companies.

Competition's win-lose paradigm, however, is being replaced. Communities and platforms not only go beyond win-lose competition but even transcend the more recent win-win paradigm. These digital communities and platforms introduce a paradigm of cocreation; and cocreation, more than any existing paradigm, makes markets surge.

The second, and even more dangerous, truth about the way traditional firms pursue agility and digital reinvention: The professed new and improved methods for accelerating agility are largely optimized *from the past* and *for the past*—meaning these frameworks are applied to the ways businesses and IT teams have been building software since the last computer revolution of the early 1990s.

You don't have to be an IT professional or software geek to understand that any breakthrough in digital that occurred over 20 years ago is a relic. But what you might not know (and this is critically important) is that today's headlines about the digital revolution harbor a dirty little secret—namely, that most traditional companies mislead themselves and others when they claim progress toward digital transformation and the cloud. In contrast to ExOs, most large firms today are just lifting and shifting their 1990s-style apps and running them in the cloud.

Although there may be an incremental economic lift from this approach, it does nothing to advance the agility and innovation of the organization, nor does it do anything to transform the company. In other words, it doesn't prepare organizations for the technical and customer transformations that are already in motion, driven by cloud-native companies.

PARADIGM SHIFT:
DIGITAL WAVES AND LIVING SYSTEMS

In our work to help large companies and executives plan, initiate, and navigate digital transformation, there is almost always a reflective pause in the conversation when they are walked through our Digital Wave Model (a model we'll unpack in Chapter 2). They can't help but appreciate how the technology and process improvements espoused by today's agile and DevOps movements are built largely on the 1990s computing paradigm of client-server. But when shown the Cloud-Native Paradigm, they see a radically different model and a correspondingly different business design and culture, one that can be used to leapfrog industry peers. The Digital Wave Model describes how and why ExOs operate with unrivaled speed to leverage their advantages over traditional companies.

So how big a deal is the Cloud-Native Paradigm? From the start, ExOs were conceived and designed to exploit the innovations and agility the cloud provides. Geeky sounding things like IaaS (Infrastructure as a Service), PaaS (Platform as a Service), SaaS (Software as a Service), and APIs (Application Programming Interfaces) are a foundational part of the "secret sauce" that enables these firms to innovate, pivot, and grow at rates never before seen from traditional firms. Cloud to them is the new canvas of business, providing the tools for rapidly experimenting and discovering new ways to engage customers and deliver novel solutions. This shift from fragile yet unwieldy software platforms (something referred to as "monoliths") to rapid, Lego block style plug-and-play software fabrication (something called Microservices) is the new creative pallet ExO leaders are using to disrupt and reshape entire industries.

To understand what they have achieved, one needs to appreciate that this revolutionary paradigm enables frictionless, continuous deployment of new digital products and customer experiences by placing powerful design and orchestration tools in the hands of small, autonomous teams.

Let's start by asking: Why small autonomous teams? The adoption of lean and agile practices focuses on establishing small, autonomous teams as the means for improving performance and employee satisfaction because this produces a more adaptive organizational structure (even while it requires a corporate commitment, feedback from local managers, and learning and development resources for team members[2]).

Orchestration tools and cloud platforms allow autonomous teams to experiment effortlessly and recombine thousands of smaller services at scale without burdensome coordinating structures and bureaucratic project management. In this environment, teams are more entrepreneurial and think innovatively about how business models and business processes are integrated into technology and customer experience. In other words, this paradigm isn't only an IT or tech play; it is a *business* play.

The payoff? The Cloud-Native Paradigm enables ExOs to execute with one-tenth of the workforce and at a hundred times the speed of traditional companies![3]

---

2   James Hess. *Empowering Autonomous Teams.* https://iveybusinessjournal.com/publication/empowering-autonomous-teams/

3   Salim Ismail, *Exponential Organizations: Why New Organizations Are Ten Times Better, Faster, and Cheaper than Yours (and What to Do about It)*, with Michael S. Malone and Yuri van Geest (New York: Diversion Books, 2014).

Working with large, traditional enterprises, we have discovered how to avoid the lift and shift trap. The emerging digital landscape (which is covered in Section I) requires traditional enterprises to calibrate their journey based on foundational building blocks (Section II). This produces a unique combination of roadmap and dynamic playbook designed specifically for your company, one that starts with your existing organizational structure and processes (*start where you are*), and leverages the people and culture that are the heart and mind of your company to propel you forward (*follow yes*).

With such powerful outcomes at stake, however, executives nonetheless become discouraged when they learn about how ExOs use cloud-native platforms to outcompete, out-innovate, and outgrow traditional firms; why? On the one hand, executives often get stuck in the glittering short-term successes of moving from waterfall to agile. More obviously and significantly they struggle to visualize how the technical and commercial benefits of platforms and microservices can be incorporated into their current organizational structure.

To compound the problem, while some leaders realize that process or automation improvements alone will never close the gap between cloud-native companies and their own companies, others think that adopting agile or DevOps will automatically level the playing field. Additionally, some leaders resist the idea that 20+ years of investment in their organizational culture, management practices, organizational structures, and computing paradigm must all be radically reshaped to catch up. In all such cases, executives fail to break the comforting bonds of their old mental models. The result is that the biggest challenge is likely not one of technology adoption but one of imagination, i.e., being able to influence systemic change across the human dimensions of organizational operation and corporate culture.

If conventional approaches to digital transformation were our subject here, we would agree that enabling your company to leap to cloud-native agility and beyond would be impossible. But *Surge* is *not* about a way to improve the *conventions* of corporate change and transformation; nor is it about the linear, mechanistic approach to agile or lean transformation. No, our approach is a journey built on a paradigm shift in how companies learn and see themselves. Fundamental to our approach is a move toward seeing companies as living systems, not machines.

Once companies embody this new vision of themselves, their living system, one composed of creative people, they are freed up to harness previously untapped social forces and to innovate. Tapping these resources, however, means stepping outside the confines of an org chart, outside of the familiar habits of command-and-control leadership, and outside of bureaucratic management practice—and then stepping into the living and breathing "hairball" that describes complex adaptive systems.

In this new way of reanimating your organization for digital, transformation isn't exclusively about adopting shiny new technology; it's more about enabling the organization to organically recognize, mobilize, and adapt to the opportunities that technology represents. It is this very competency of listening, learning, and adapting that makes ExOs so successful, and, if you're willing, this same power to listen, learn, and adapt to the living system of your organization is available . . . and obtainable right now.

OUR APPROACH:
START WHERE YOU ARE AND FOLLOW YES

Despite more than a decade of so-called "breakthrough agile thinking and methods," very little in the way of authentic company-wide agility and reinvention has occurred in traditional companies. It is this harsh truth that motivated us to pursue discovery of a better, more systemic way to transform traditional companies for digital, beginning with three foundational assumptions:

1. Organizations are *networks of people, ecosystems* that evolve over time, and they function more like biological systems than like machines.

2. Networks of people behave like *complex adaptive systems*, thriving when lightly controlled and suffering when burdened by heavy structure and intensive management.

3. Even the oldest, most rigid command-and-control corporations are not broken or "sick," and therefore cannot be "fixed" in the traditional sense; they are holistic systems that may be functioning perfectly, *even if the attributes of the current system are undesirable.*

These assumptions have changed the questions we've asked ourselves and our clients. They've also altered the way we've challenged our clients' legacy patterns for organizing.

Over the years, we have developed techniques to help large enterprises create new digital strategies. As we probed, provoked, and disrupted these organizations, designing new practices, discarding old frameworks, and learning from diverse thinkers, clarity was gained about the digital wave journey—that is, about the ways in which waves of digital technologies impact the whole enterprise, not just technology teams. And frankly, the deep interplay that must happen between the new digital technologies being developed and the underlying organizational structures, culture, and practices continues to amaze us.

If we've uncovered one nearly universal truth, it is this: The speed and the success of moving your company through its unique digital journey are governed not by your investment in new technology and tools, but by the pace at which your organization can jettison old beliefs and habits and foster new ones *in their place*.

To be clear, what we urge is not another change initiative. Most change initiatives fail — about 70 percent. Instead, what we urge is total reinvention. Chronically bound to the past, change initiatives seek to maintain and optimize the traditional company structure. They tinker, not transform. Reinvention, on the other hand, is nothing less than a phoenix experience. To transform, you must disrupt and destabilize your living ecosystem, encouraging it to self-organize into something new, even something unexpected. This takes deep trust in yourself and others.

Of course, reinvention demands massive energy. At the same time, reinvention inspires curiosity and engagement, which together breathe new life into the corporate ecosystem.

What emerged from our work was a new sense-making tool: The Digital Wave Model. This tool helps companies first to recognize and then to develop the relationship among technology, culture, and organizational design.

We understand now how organizations transform from the legacy of industrial-age management, structure, and culture to the DNA of digital natives. Moreover, we recognize — and you will too — that transformation involves difficult, challenging choices that require technical and business stakeholders to learn not just how to work with each other, but also how to emerge as a more cohesive whole, as members of the same team. This means each stakeholder must subvert or lose part of his or her individual identity in order to build a coalesced joint identity.

Unlike large consultancies that swarm in on an enterprise and deliver a prepackaged roadmap, we believe that the answers every enterprise seeks are internal. You will learn to see your organization as a living system, a dynamic whole that interacts with itself and with market ecosystems. From this perspective, your organization is not broken, so it's not really a question of "fixing" it. In fact, living systems tend to have their own solutions embedded within them; embedded yes, but often dormant. Unleashing the latent creativity already present in your company will discourage formulaic prescription and instead be more diagnostic.

To help companies uncover and link up these hidden solutions, we begin with organizational anthropology, interviewing people and observing, among other things, meetings, internal conversations, and team members working together.

Asking people why they do what they do, exploring otherwise unquestioned habits and underlying assumptions, we look for mental models, norms, and culture, which include artifacts in the environment. Then we ask how problems are solved and how decisions are made, which leads to finding out who has the power and how he or she uses (or abuses) it.

In short, rather than bringing in hordes of consultants and slide decks, utilize people in the organization — which unleashes the creative power already within a company! In these pages you will find no single framework that applies to all organizations. We want you first to understand where you are so that you can get to where you want to be.

Embrace the following mantra: *Start where you are and follow yes.*

USING SURGE

Remember that this is a voyage that the organization *must* take *because digital transformation is not a bolt-on program, but a complete reinvention of the organization itself.* When we refer to digital transformation, we are not merely talking about software; we are talking about hyperconnectivity.

Hyperconnectivity poses unparalleled challenges that are changing your competitors, customers, and stakeholders. If organizations
believe the fantasy that digital hyperconnectivity doesn't apply to
them, then they will not survive these waves; others will take surely
their place in the market. The evidence of this over the last 10 years
is indisputable.

This book is organized into two sections. Section I dives into the
foundations of digital transformation, exploring what you need to
know about the challenges you face, as well as the characteristics of
each digital wave.

Section II details the journey of digital transformation. Used
effectively, the elements we outline replace the dysfunctional legacy
of business as order placer and IT as order taker with an emergent
model of cross-disciplinary networks capable of learning, executing,
and innovating at the speed of digital.

The Digital Wave Model determines where your company stands
in relation to the next transformation. The journey of digital transformation provides actionable advice for you to make the changes
your company needs. Together, *Surge* provides you and your company the means for navigating the extreme forces that digital transformation introduces to human, organizational, and technical
systems. Among others, *Surge* is for people who work in large companies that are not yet exponential organizations. This includes companies with 500–1,000+ employees, companies where bureaucratic
friction often prevails.

Although *Surge* is rich in practicality, to avoid prescription we offer
conceptual frameworks and practices that you can use to tailor the
reinvention of your current situation. For those of you interested in
learning more, visit www.surgetoolkit.com for an in-depth exploration of these ideas that is continuously updated.

We acknowledge that hierarchy can sometimes hamper digital

transformation, but it is not the main adversary. With its entrenched rules and processes, bureaucracy (not hierarchy) is the true enemy of digital transformation.

Surge is a guide to help you recognize and catch your inbound digital wave, whether it is adopting agile or augmented intelligence. It includes the background you need to generate your own experiments and to test your own ideas. We are constantly sharing updates to existing approaches, new ideas, and further evidence of success, so be sure to visit our Surge website regularly to learn more.

Make no mistake: There is no avoiding the digital waves. You can hunker down within your current wave and keep doing the same things incrementally faster and cheaper, but not better. Or you can face the waves head-on, seeing them as constructive challenges and as creative opportunities to make what currently seems impossible become possible.

We live in exciting times. Today's companies and markets face transformations akin to those the agricultural era faced at the dawn of the Industrial Revolution. Computers, software, and the Internet have transformed and will continue to transform our global business landscape, just like steam, electricity, and cheap labor did in the Nineteenth Century. If you are ready to face the digital waves and willing to learn how to navigate them, turn the page.

Surge is for you.

"The whole idea that a map can be drawn in advance of an innovative journey through turbulent times is a fantasy . . . Route and destination must be discovered through the journey itself if you wish to travel to new lands. The key to success lies in the creative activity of making new maps, not in the imitative following and refining of existing ones."

—Ralph Stacey, *Managing the Unknowable*

THE FOUNDATIONS OF DIGITAL TRANSFORMATION

When Pitney Bowes was founded in 1920, the disruptive consumer gadgets of the day included washing machines, vacuum cleaners, and refrigerators, transforming the domestic lives of middle-class families around the world. Pitney Bowes's contribution to innovation that same year was the world's first commercial postage meter. Some might find it ironic that the company most known for bringing innovations to physical mail delivery is today a digital leader, except for one thing: Pitney Bowes has reinvented itself more than five times in the last 100 years.

In fact, Pitney Bowes is an example of a company that reinvents itself again and again in the face of disruptive technological change. Consider the following milestones of Pitney Bowes' journey of reinvention over the last 100 years:

1920 First Commercial Postage Meter
1957 Mail-Sorting Automation
1968 First Bar Code Reading Machine for Retail
1978 Pioneering of Electronic Funds Transfer
         ("Postage by Phone")
1986 Intelligent Fax Machines for Business
1998 Secure Digital Document Delivery
2007 Real-Time Location-Logistics Intelligence
2014 Pitney Bowes Commerce Cloud

As Internet and global connectivity has soared through the 2000s, Pitney Bowes has had no choice but to reinvent yet again. What makes the company's story so instructive is that Pitney Bowes didn't approach reinvention as a break from the customers they serve, but instead as a *complete reimagining of how to serve those customers*. They spent decades positioning themselves to be the dominant provider of commerce intelligence for future customers—and continue doing so to this day.

Pitney Bowes knew one thing better than anyone else: The business of shipping and logistics was ripe for transformation, not just optimization. Applying their deep knowledge and experience, Pitney Bowes didn't seek to use cloud technologies and agile execution to make their offerings and business more efficient, they instead imagined an entirely new operating model from the ground up. In doing so they launched their own Commerce Cloud. This new platform for enabling clients to acquire real-time customer insights, ship physical products, communicate, and facilitate payments is so effective that today's largest digital native companies consider Commerce Cloud essential to their success.

For instance, eBay relies on Commerce Cloud to confirm international shipping availability and pricing, and Twitter and Zillow rely on Pitney Bowes to confirm the physical location of over one billion consumers active on social media. This shift from a legacy mailing automation company to a cloud-based intelligence, business, and commerce platform demonstrates how different authentic digital and agile transformation is from the legacy business/IT operating models that still exist in many large firms today. The fact that Pitney Bowes has made such shifts not just once, or even a handful of times, but over and over again through the last 100 years, proves that navigating the Age of Surge is not limited to only those who call themselves "digital natives."

Let's look at another example, this time a corporation disrupted by external factors. In 2006 the venerable *Washington Post* not only celebrated its 129th birthday, but also recorded its all-time highest annual revenue: 962 million dollars. Since then, though, the *Post*—indeed, the entire print newspaper industry—has been in free fall. While Google and Facebook advertising growth has come at the expense of newspaper display advertising, the story gets even more bleak when you consider that, on average, over 40 percent of newspaper revenues traditionally came from classified ads, a source of income that will never return.

In 1995 a programmer named Craig Newmark was laid off from his job at Charles Schwab. With the help of a modest severance package, Newmark started a free email list service to promote art events in the San Francisco area. Less than a year later the service evolved into Craigslist, a community-based host for peer-to-peer ads of all kinds. Classified ad listings at craigslist.org are free, there are no word limits, and it's easy to create an ad. Craigslist offers the best of the print world *through* the much better and more relevant digital advertising/delivery medium: Unlike newspaper classifieds, Craigslist ads are published instantly and are available to anyone with a web browser. By 2000, for-sale listings on Craigslist had gutted nearly all classified ad revenues of newspapers across the country.[1]

---

1 https://www.forbes.com/sites/jeffbercovici/2013/08/14/sorry-craig-study-finds-craigslist-cost-newspapers-5-billion/#13f9f5517d02

Employment ads were the next classifieds to go. During the 1999 Super Bowl, two upstart Internet firms, Monster.com and Hot-Jobs, ran Super Bowl ads promoting their online job search services. Again, online jobs listings offered advantages traditional classified employment ads could not match, including easy communication, wide dissemination, and instant publication. Craigslist had devastated classified ads by offering individual sellers a new way to connect with buyers; Monster.com and HotJobs similarly offered employers an alternative to newspaper employment ads, gutting yet another major source of newspaper revenues.

The rise of digital natives like Craigslist and Monster.com has obviously been devastating to traditional print newspapers; what can they do without those vital revenues? From 2006 to 2013, the *Washington Post* saw its revenues decline by nearly half, to an estimated $506 million in 2013, and the paper lost a staggering $400 million during that period.

Still, while the numbers would seem to suggest otherwise, the *Post* was not asleep at the wheel. In fact, the paper initiated a number of strategic initiatives in 2008, including a move to retool its technology and IT operations to a fully agile delivery and operating model. The move to agile was declared a success in 2010, but the company continued to hemorrhage cash and suffer record declines in revenue.

In 2013, as the *Post* teetered on the verge of financial collapse, Jeff Bezos, the founder of Amazon, offered to buy the paper for $250 million cash. It was, to say the least, a surprising move. But where most saw in the print news industry accelerating irrelevance, Bezos saw the potential to reimagine the newspaper business for a world gone digital. He saw an opportunity for the *Post* to envision an entirely new version of itself, one that preserved its unique value of high quality journalism while making it relevant in and to the new terrain of digital.

While the transformation initiated by Bezos's acquisition is still a work in progress, the early results are eye opening: The *Post* has doubled its web visitor traffic — it now attracts a monthly following that exceeds that of the *New York Times*, an early adopter of digital in the newspaper world — and it now publishes more daily news reports (written by its own journalists) than many digital-native news outlets, including *Buzzfeed*. More recently, it has given birth to a thriving high-margin software business that emerged from the *Post's* pursuing new ways to empower journalists to consume, synthesize, and publish high-impact news for the web. Solving this problem for themselves, the *Post* has discovered a lucrative, entirely new source of income for the paper that is projected to generate more than $100 million a year in recurring revenue.

What's more, the *Post* achieved these successes in just three years, *while remaining* true to its core business of news and journalism. In other words, in redefining the company for the digital age, Bezos didn't seek to kill off its core business — and core identity. Nor did he jettison what he saw as its assets, like its leadership team. The *Post's* emerging transformational story includes the critical contributions of two of the paper's leaders: Joey Marburger, who acts as the paper's director of product, and Shailesh Prakash, the Chief Product and Technology Officer, both of whom had been with the *Post* well before Bezos acquired the paper. In other words: same leaders, same organization, but radically different (better!) results.

Instead of hollowing out the company and making it something else, Bezos challenged the paper's leadership to stop using technology merely to optimize what the paper had always been and done, and instead to imagine an entirely new way to exploit the unique strengths of the venerable news organization (the paper is more than 140 years old) for the digital era. This latter choice is in direct opposition to conventional wisdom among tech and business pundits: That large-scale digital transformation is certain to fail without wholesale changes to leadership and a comprehensive, well-conceived roadmap. The *Post*'s transformation occurred without either of these "must haves," so the obvious questions become: What was the source of the impressive transformation? Did Bezos simply copy the things that worked at Amazon and install them at the *Post*; did he start by fixing everything that was "wrong" with the *Post*; or did he come to his solution in other ways?

Certainly the similarities between the digital news business and e-commerce give Bezos an advantage, things like: increasing website speed, mobile apps, personalized recommendations, and social media. But the answer to the above "yes or no" questions is a resounding "No." Instead, like all leaders whose companies are successfully navigating the disruption wrought by digital, Bezos acknowledged and amplified the fundamental truth of business in the digital age. In an open letter to *Washington Post* employees upon his purchase of the paper in 2013, Bezos had this to say about the path forward: "There is no map, and charting a path ahead will not be easy. We will need to invent, which means we will need to experiment."[2]

In other words, digital transformation is an improvisational journey, not a scripted roadmap. And what Bezos didn't change is as important as what he is changing. His speech during the dedication of the new *Post* building in 2016 explains, "Important institutions like the *Post* have an essence, they have a heart, they have a core—what Marty called a soul," he said. "And if you wanted that to change, you'd be crazy. That's part of what this place is, it's part of what makes it so special."[3]

---

2 https://www.washingtonpost.com/national/jeff-bezos-on-post-purchase/2013/08/05/e5b293de-fe0d-11e2-9711-3708310f6f4d_story.html?utm_term=.b7be8f8dc58f

3 https://shorensteincenter.org/bezos-effect-washington-post/

Finally, as to "What was the source of the impressive transformation of *Washington Post* and Pitney Bowes?": While they have forged a path toward complete reinvention of their core business and operating models, most companies today are settling for more tactical improvements, using agile execution and cloud to merely optimize the businesses they're already in. The *Washington Post* and Pitney Bowes have exploited digital technology to disrupt both themselves and the markets they serve. They see today's digital waves and agile tools not just as means for driving efficiency and speed, but as sources of organizational tension, innovation, and reinvention.

The most important extension upon this idea that *any* company can make today is that the secrets of digital reinvention are not for the sacred few, but for everyone! And the first step is as easy as: "Start Where You Are, and Follow Yes." This is at the heart of transformation, and is foundational to *the* key points we'll explore in this section: Understanding digital transformation and navigating the digital wave journey.

Chapter 1

Start Where You Are

When a powerful dust storm hits Mars in the movie *The Martian*, the fictional crew of *Ares III* is forced to evacuate the habitat station on the planet. The members rush to their ship, but astronaut Mark Watney is lost in the storm. As the storm escalates, Commander Lewis makes the difficult decision to leave Mark behind to save the rest of the crew. The group launches to its orbiting ship while they mourn the loss of their crewmate and friend, and NASA is alerted to his death.

The next morning Mark wakes up to a calm Mars. He winces and looks down, seeing an antenna has pierced his abdomen. A hole in a space suit usually means death, but luckily the antenna and the blood from his wound have created a seal that is keeping his oxygen from escaping his suit, though he is running low. Mark slowly and painfully walks to the habitat station. Once inside, he first performs minor surgery on himself to remove the antenna and then sets about figuring out how he'll survive on Mars.

In a video log, he details his problems. He is stranded with no way to contact Earth. Moreover, the next planetary mission to Mars won't be for another four years, yet he has just one year's supply of food. He also has to figure out how to make water on a planet with no water source.

Over the next few months Mark uses his expertise in botany and mechanical engineering to stay alive. He grows a potato farm inside the habitat using human fertilizer and Martian soil. He burns hydrazine rocket fuel to make water. He eventually figures out how to communicate with NASA through instant chat and works with them to plan his rescue. When an explosion compromises the habitat, he reseals the airlock with duct tape and devises a new plan.[1] We'll stop the spoilers there, in case you haven't read the book or watched the movie.

In *The Martian* Mark Watney deals with the real constraints present in his world and continuously moves forward. His only mission is to survive, and to do that he has to acknowledge the reality and risks of his present situation. As constraints keep tightening, he has to respond . . . or die.

"No matter what happens," he says, "tell the world, tell my family, I never stopped fighting to make it home."[2]

Two things aid Mark's survival. First, he embraces the reality of his situation. He knows he will die unless he works within the confines of his situation. Second, he looks at his predicament with a new frame of reference, a new mental model. He lists all the things he has, but instead of seeing a packet of dehydrated potatoes and rocket

1 "Synopsis for *The Martian* (2015)," IMDB, accessed May 3, 2017, http://www.imdb. com/title/tt3659388/synopsis?ref_=ttpl_pl_syn.

2 20th Century Fox, "*The Martian* | Official Trailer [HD] | 20th Century FOX," YouTube video, 03:08, August 19, 2015, https://www.youtube.com/watch?v= ej3ioOneTy8.

fuel, he sees a potato farm and water. He's able to reenvision his few
assets as possibilities and to imagine novel ways to repurpose things
in his environment in order to survive.

What Mark and the people working from Earth to save him do
is put into practice the maxim *start where you are and follow yes*. This is
also the central precept we use to help enterprise leaders transform
their organizations.

Mark starts with the constraint that he is stranded on Mars, and
he then works within every additional constraint his reality continues to reveal. Individuals at NASA join in to help, "following yes"
and saying, "I'll be responsible for this part of saving Mark." Each
person works tirelessly for the mission. Operating together, people who can — and must — help, act. Meanwhile, Mark is drawing
from the past, working with every feasible resource he can think of
in the present, and focusing on the future.

Transformation in your enterprise is a critical mission in its own
right. As with Mark and NASA, it all begins with knowing where
you are, i.e., the initial conditions and constraints that you have to
work with; if these factors go unrecognized, they *will* threaten your
survival. All too often legacy companies look at their organizations
with their collective eyes fixed on the past, asking, *What have we done to
solve these kinds of problems before?*

Because there is no road map for digital transformation, information that focuses on the past can be dangerous, particularly
when it emphasizes best practices from past successes. This retro-
spective approach is hazardous because it fails to emphasize context, your unique conditions and constraints. We are all currently
operating at a time when the answers of the past have already been
made irrelevant by ever-increasing digital advances; this *must* be
recognized and acknowledged.

In fact, digital first movers radically redefine today's market context in real time. As you read these words, new breakthroughs are being made and turned into products and services. Although we can draw principles from technical success stories, replication will never be the answer because the solutions of the past, even the very recent past, were designed for a different context, a different company, a different market or industry, a different world.

For these reasons progressive companies are investing in digital to safeguard their future. Leaders must now view transforming to a digital enterprise as *the* area to invest in if they're going to have not only current viability, but long-term relevance and sustainability in their industries and markets. Along the way businesses must realize that, although technology is a crucial part of digital transformation, by itself it is an incomplete solution. For without the personal and organizational transformations that go with it, new digital technologies are little more than shiny tools used alongside decaying organizational structures and processes — and their usefulness cannot be maximized.

YOU AREN'T GOOGLE — YOU ARE YOU

Books and articles about exponential growth and digital leaders almost always look at the best practices of digital natives. The remarkable stories of Google, Netflix, and Amazon abound. However, the strategies these companies have employed to scale digital innovation can't be used *as is* on organizations that were founded on older business designs. Current and imminent situations change from organization to organization. That is why saying, "I want to be like Google" will never work.

And, honestly, you don't want to be like Google . . . because *you are not Google.*

Although it may be easier to try being like someone else, you must figure out what it means to be yourself. You must do the hard, dirty work of understanding where you are—and where *your yes* is and should be taking you.

Hundred-year-old companies reached the century mark because they reinvented themselves over and over *as only they could.* Digital transformation means understanding where you, and only you, are starting from. Strategically, begin by looking at your market and industry to understand the changes coming your way. In the organizational sphere, examine your culture, your brand, your identity, and understand your customers' ways of living in this new world. In the technical sphere, see beyond specific software code or new tools. In the ecosphere, perceive your whole system: the entire human enterprise.

Starting where you are begins with questions: What is the purpose of your company? What is your current reality? What are your constraints? What do you want to achieve? Starting where you are demands awareness, recognizing the constraints as well as the assets in front of you, and using them in your digital transformation journey. Knowing where you are is a must to help you make timely decisions as you transform.

Starting where you are also means recognizing that while the system you're in functions perfectly from a systems perspective, to change you have to disrupt the system, destabilize it, and allow it to restabilize into new ways of functioning. Creative destruction and creative regeneration work by shaking loose old habits, mindsets, connections, and boundaries that are keeping you from transformation and exponential growth.

Once you recognize where you are, it's time to identify and remove the critical bottlenecks that slow or derail your transformation. There are three that we typically encounter:

First, don't make the digital transformation a project or initiative in only one part of the corporation. This is going to apply to the whole company and needs to be addressed by everyone. Even if they are not immediately engaged in technical or organizational change, all employees should be aware of the digital strategy. (This, of course, implies that the highest-level leaders have a strategy and are personally committed to it — though that is sometimes not the case.).

Understand that digital transformation will take several years to be completed. This alone requires investment of human and financial resources. For the groups that go through the transformation first (typically in business or product chunks), investment and support for nine to twelve months allow them to make significant headway. Remember that they are designing and building a new ship while sailing the one they're on and then decommissioning the old craft, reusing what resources they can. These first movers reveal the tightly coupled processes and structures that are impediments you must remove. Which brings us to the second bottleneck.

Once they are revealed, you have to triage and tackle the most critical and systemic corporate problems. There are obvious ones in every organization: demand and/or change management, finance, resource allocation processes, and centralized planning and decision-making (if they still exist). Digital transformation integrates technical teams into the business, requiring new skill sets and ways of working. As slow, bulky business requirement documents are eliminated, technical teams take on responsibility for building *products* end-to-end, rather than delivering projects with limited functionality. Removing this bottleneck requires constructing missing feedback loops between customers and business, business and technology, and different business units (enabling the capture of synergies).

The third bottleneck is your outdated architecture, the monoliths that are currently powering your company. This involves a delicate balancing act: knowing where you are headed and what it could look like when you get there, *and* not letting technology outpace the business and organizational transformation that must occur along the way. Technological transformation is easy to define. Business and organizational transformation is not; it is not only difficult to define, but it can be messy, and it is very human. It is emotional and requires significant behavioral change at all levels of the organization. No one is exempt!

As processes and ways to engage with customers change, so too do the options for structuring the organization. Unlike the industrial transformation, which encouraged homogeneity, digital transformation encourages diversity. There are multiple ways of structuring the digital businesses within a corporation to meet the needs of customers. Businesses must avoid the trap of imposing a single structure, method, or set of tools and processes during transformation, and let experimentation at the onset (divergence) reveal what works best in the company, before convergence naturally occurs.

Following yes is a natural outgrowth of starting where you are. It reinforces existing positive action at the same time as it helps you identify new actions you must take. To begin, look for people and opportunities that are already surging forward. Find individuals in your organization who are thinking and acting in ways that can make your digital transformation a reality.

At its heart, following yes is about a sincere willingness to leave your current state, the status quo. It's about building momentum. Most of our clients are large corporations filled with thousands of people with great ideas who are doing small, local experiments that few people know about. We help these clients connect people with great ideas and form a network of digital innovators.

In one case, we connected managers from two operations groups working with completely different products and services, and we established a peer-to-peer coaching network. The managers faced different technical challenges, but their organizational challenges were the same. Both groups were experimenting with agile but approaching it in different ways. Their new relationships enabled them to coach each other with understanding, provide insights, and help each other identify actions they could take. For these managers, committing themselves to coaching was a wonderful example of following yes.

Following yes also means disrupting the whole company so that the early adopters can be found and transformed. Again, three things turn this approach into a transformation backlog, in other words, a prioritized book of work that turns transformational ideas into action:

First, a company needs to remove the middle clay layers of information hoarding and management resistance. In bloated, bureaucratic enterprises middle managers are at risk of losing their jobs. Rather than ignoring this and allowing it to become a major bottleneck, they need to be engaged. We find that acknowledging that their role and work will dramatically change *and* confirming that they will continue to have a critical role to play begins their transformation. We begin by engaging all middle managers in an adaptive leadership program not only to change their mindset and behavior, but also because they impact all the people they touch. When they themselves begin challenging the status quo and participating in conversations that define the future, intentional disruption of the organization has begun. (We cover this in-depth in Section II.)

One reason we like this technique is that it reveals the positive deviants in your company (see sidebar), the second action of following yes. Who are the positive deviants? And how do you find them?

Virtually every company has employees whose ideas and approaches to the adoption of new technology and the organizational challenges it unleashes produce successful new behaviors

In addition to its impact on the digital wave journey, we find
positive deviance particularly appealing for the following reasons:

~ Positive deviance is a strengths-based approach.

~ It applies to problems that require behavioral and social
  change along with technical and process rewiring.

~ It assumes that the company contains the answer, and is not
  broken and needing to be fixed.

~ It finds solutions to transformational challenges within
  the company.

~ It recognizes that employees are the best experts to solve
  their own problems.

~ It sees companies as living systems that have the capability to
  self-organize, using resources and social assets to collectively
  resolve their most pressing issues (i.e., they are self-healing).

~ It emphasizes that it is easier to change behavior by
  addressing it in the context of daily challenges, and that the
  answer lies inside the organization, not outside it.

and strategies. Deviant thinkers routinely find better solutions
to challenges and opportunities than their peers, despite contex-
tual similarities (e.g., culture, position, and experience). In fact,
positive deviants find solutions despite having no extra resources
or knowledge. They tend to solve for persistent and widespread
problems, creating solutions that, once identified and harnessed,
can benefit the whole company. Finding your positive deviants is
a matter of watching for those who disrupt the system *and* cause
it to stabilize at a higher level of performance — not an easy task,
but well worth the effort.

For example, one executive we've worked with is a positive deviant who is constantly assessing and applying novel analytics to the human systems within his organization, which is part of a large media company. On his own he designed tools for tracking individual and group performance more effectively. He devised a way to analyze how three groups in his technical division could measure and coordinate their activities to build a cohesive platform that created value when the opportunity was high but the time short.

The third aspect of operationalizing follow yes is establishing a test-and-learn approach to transformation. Acknowledge that there is no one method, that you are learning as you transform. It will surprise you how quickly business leaders will raise their hands to take on digital transformation. It is then up to you to choose your first groups based on leadership bench strength, the ability to generate game-changing customer and business value, and enough complexity so that you can identify and change the organizational bottlenecks that apply to everyone.

Importantly, this means that you can start only as many groups as you can support until they can support themselves and maintain momentum. Because they are going to be changing iteratively and fast, your support team has to continuously learn and change as well. It won't help you that they are agile experts if they can't learn to be lean experts, product experts, and organizational experts as well. Consider how you are going to ramp up your transformation and make it sustainable without bringing in swarms of external help. This is a chance for displaced individuals to find a new home, so consider things like coaching academies, training facilitators for the new techniques you'll be using, and train-the-trainer programs to expand your transformational capacity.

Digital transformation means you're ready to make the decision to leave the status quo: You have a directional idea of where

you *want* to go, where you *need* to go, and you've *decided* to go. You
know that you may need to take a detour here and there, which
is not only okay, but often helpful. But if you haven't committed
to the decision, even if you have the readiness, then you are not
yet following yes. Companies who follow yes do not place large
prerequisites ahead of initiating the journey. To impose prerequisites is to miss opportunities. They do not wait for conditions that
will be ideal for achieving the outcomes they desire; instead, they
create those conditions. Unburdened by their current state, they
overcome inertia, they get moving, and they learn how to correct
their course as they go.

And transformation has a ripple effect. People see a problem,
and they think, *Someone needs to do something about this, . . . and that someone should be me!* This spawns a culture of accountability and innovation. Once one group starts to transform, others tend to join them,
and they begin to attract the resources they need. As groups link
up, they in turn transform culture. Suddenly, across the organization, there exists the positive pull of people who have great ideas and
want them to be valued and used. Identify these change agents and
amplify their insights.

In every social system, people follow norms and contribute to
strongly held beliefs. Social science research shows that when *around
12 percent* of a group begin to think differently about a prevailing idea,
moving the whole social system becomes possible. Think about that.
You need only *12–15 percent* of your organization to change its perspective,[3] then attitudes, behaviors, and actions shift, a process we
call *transformation in place* (TIP).[4]

---

3 This is also true for customers, markets, and societies and is fueling the
   digital revolution.

4 Thanks to Mel Conway for this language.

TIP means that you don't have to convince everybody of the need for digital transformation. Instead, you need only to invest your energy in the people who are already interested. That small group will grow, sharing their experiences with others, and suddenly you will exceed small percentages . . . and watch as TIP gains momentum.

Organizational systems that undergo TIP have a productive relationship with volatility, uncertainty, complexity, and ambiguity (VUCA), which positions them at the edge of chaos.

VUCA AND THE EDGE OF CHAOS

Organizations are alive, teeming with human energy. Like natural ecosystems, they are dynamic and active, functioning as an old-growth forest or a healthy body. An ecosystem, at its simplest, is a system composed of autonomous elements, individuals in an organization, that interact with each other and the environment, creating a dynamic that is capable of both stability and change. It is structured as a network of subsystems woven together by their relationships. Ecosystems are always in flux, reshaped by the information and resources flowing through them. They emerge based on two fundamentals: first, who participates in the ecosystem, and second, the order in which they join. Get these right and the ecosystem will generate vast numbers of products and services, as well as amazing amounts of value.

These living systems operate far from a state of equilibrium, thriving at "the edge of chaos." Companies too must operate far from a state of equilibrium if they are to adapt quickly to market changes while maintaining organizational coherence. By transforming parts of the organization rather than merely optimizing them for current conditions, companies are better able to survive the shifting tides of market evolution.

And while the edge of chaos appears volatile, at that edge adaptation establishes *dynamic stability*. If you look at the transformation process, parts of the organization seem to be on the brink of unraveling, particularly when the process is functioning as it should (meaning when no single individual controls it). Yet the chaos has a hidden order, and, over time, the shift from volatile to stable emerges. Paradoxically, volatility of the parts establishes stability of the whole, and dynamic stability generates adaptation of the entire system.

Transformation challenges organizations to act beyond their current experiences, capabilities, and comfort zones. And as the magnitude of change grows, its receptiveness to being controlled declines. Successful enterprises amplify the energy and enthusiasm of change agents and create the conditions for them to thrive, making their organizations more likely to complete their transformation. This process continually introduces VUCA, which feeds the edge of chaos cycle.

Volatility, uncertainty, complexity, and ambiguity — these four elements of VUCA — are also four fundamental elements you must embrace as you embark on your digital transformation journey, especially since they will be with you the entire way. Let's unpack VUCA to see how to use it to your benefit, not just experience its disruption.

Each element of VUCA *reveals* an organizational blind spot impacting your culture, leadership, and operating models (Table 1.1). For example, volatility reveals where you are vulnerable. Due to our mental models and assumptions about the world, market, or company, we don't often know our vulnerabilities; but we can *resolve* volatility by becoming more vigilant, introducing behaviors and activities that search for weak signals, encourage mindfulness, identify and question our assumptions, and update them when changes in the environment occur. Vigilance — searching out vulnerability that leads to volatility — reduces the number of surprises you have to respond to, decreasing shoot-from-the-hip reactions, and building the muscles of resiliency.

Table I.I: **VUCA — The Reality of Systemic Change**

LEARNING	REVEALS	ADDRESSED BY
Volatility	Vulnerability	Vigilance
Uncertainty	Unexpected	Understanding
Complexity	Consequences	Containment
Ambiguity	Assumptions	Agility

Uncertainty plays a growing role in business today because industrial-age management is built on certainty and predictability. Management believes that market and organizational uncertainty is harmful and to be avoided at all costs. It also has an irrational expectation that certainty and predictability are possible in most cases. But in the digital world this mental model is downright dangerous. Uncertainty reveals the unexpected, things that are not on your radar (things like Airbnb, Lyft, and Swipe!).

To resolve uncertainty, you have to understand the terrain or system about which you are making predictions. The more dependencies and connections in the system, the deeper the understanding you need to have and the more uncertainty you should incorporate into your planning. Even then you must develop your ability to sense when you are making decisions based on certainty, and then walk back from your beliefs.

The third element, complexity, is something we try to eliminate in software and processes, but even five humans in a room, the size of an agile team, generate significant complexity. Complexity reveals the unintended consequences contained in the system due to the relationships between its members or components. To move beyond consequences that trip us up, relational and technical, we need to see the whole system so that we can contain disruptions when they happen (because they will).

For complex human systems, containment means open, honest, and real-time collaboration and coordination, with little lag time between feedback and action. When consequences are anticipated and containment planned, the outcome is operational reliability, regardless of complex interdependencies within the system. Therefore, we refer to them as complex adaptive systems.

That leaves us with ambiguity, which is the hardest of the four to recognize. Ambiguity results from the subjective interpretation of language (Chapter 5), causing multiple definitions and understandings. Often ambiguity is the result of people drawing conclusions based on different contexts, and in all cases it arises from unclear premises.

The danger of multiple interpretations of meaning or intent is the negative relational archetype Accidental Adversaries,[5] which occurs when interpersonal conflict arises between people as a result of the organizational system, often due to role, accountability, and/or position. This archetype is rampant in corporations and especially prevalent during transformations. It is most easily resolved when the adversarial relationship is revealed to be caused by the system and not the participants. This allows the adversaries to become collaborative partners, using agility to challenge and

---

5 Mentoring Human Action developed 10 positive and negative systemic archetypes that drive systemic behaviors. MHA Institute, *Systems Thinking Course*, (Edmonton, AB: MHA Institute, 2016), http://www.mhainstitute.ca/main/portals/1/files/Systems%20Thinking%20Course.pdf.

change the assumptions hidden in the organizational system.

Assumptions arise from the predictions our brains are wired to make about how our world will react to our actions. One of the most dangerous assumptions, confirmation bias, occurs when we filter information to match our assumptions and ignore everything that disconfirms them. Cognitive agility helps us recognize and avoid the assumptions we all use to make sense of the world, thereby reducing ambiguity.

The bottom line: VUCA tells us where and how to transform our systems. The antidotes to VUCA's Volatility, Uncertainty, Complexity, and Ambiguity — that is: vigilance, understanding, containment, and agility — keep disruptions small, encourage mindfulness and thought experiments, and cultivate diversity and inclusion, in turn effecting successful decision-making and problem-solving in the digital world.

PLATFORM COMMUNITIES:
ECOSYSTEMS ARE THE FUTURE

To illustrate just how structurally different the emerging market ecosystems of digital are, let us introduce you to the Platform Manifesto, written by Sangeet Paul Choudary.[6] What the Agile Manifesto does for agile, the Platform Manifesto does for digital (see sidebar).

A platform ecosystem brings together diverse perspectives, fields, cultures, experiences, and practices. It amplifies diversity and creates autonomy and independence between the parts while enabling interdependence of the whole. It establishes a new role, the "prosumer": someone who is both a producer and a consumer of the goods and services available on the platform.

---

6 "The Platform Manifesto," 2015, http://platformed.info/the-platform-manifesto/.

The axioms of Choudary's Platform Manifesto that we've leveraged and integrated into the Surge framework:

~ The ecosystem is also the new supply chain.

~ The network effect is the new driver for scale.

~ Data is the new dollar.

~ Community management is the new human resources.

~ Curation and reputation are the new quality control.

~ User journeys are the new sales funnel.

~ Behavior design is the new loyalty program.

~ Social media feedback is the new sales commission.

~ Algorithms are the new decision makers.

~ Real-time customization is the new market research.

~ Plug and play is the new business development.

Platforms are powerful because there is *no* perfect product for everyone. The beauty of a platform is that new functionality arises from the user's ability to also be a producer, which is true for internal as well as market-facing platforms. Because there is no perfect product for everyone, platforms are not competing on the basis of better features or new tools, but on their ability to attract interesting participants and enable creative interactions among them.

This opens the door to both social and economic value creation. Participants evolve the platform based on what they want and need, attracting new users and further evolution. Each platform community is distinct, reflecting the needs, content, and relationships between users. The Wikipedia community is dramatically different from the iTunes community, which differs from Amazon's AWS community. And Facebook's constellation of products, built by allowing user communities to do much of the ideation and discovery work, has generated social products along with commercial products. The bottom line: All platforms provide value to their members.

One way platforms provide user value is in their accessibility. By their very nature, platforms are open, participative ecosystems capable of self-management, self-governance, and self-organization. Built on the principles of open-source communities, governance by a collective commons, they produce low-friction interactions between contributors. Metrics that platform communities can track include the rate at which value is generated by interactions between producers and consumers on the platform,[7] community growth, and diversity.

As far as we can see into the digital future, digital transformation will generate ecosystems whose members cocreate products and services. Add in the developing ethos of the sharing economy, and future businesses might look quite a bit different than your company looks today. Work hard to build your platform . . . then use it for everything.

Whether you build a platform or just contribute to its products and services, you will be operating in an ecosystem. Establishing an ecosystem, or contributing to one, requires a set of interpersonal skills that most companies do not encourage today: openness, trust, collaboration, and commitment. Ecosystems are communities of equals. Open-source communities are a great illustration of markets that function as ecosystems. Google's open-source initiative called Kubernetes is an excellent example of this new way of creating value and competing as a collective.

Kubernetes is a cloud-native automation framework that

---

7 Ibid.

radically simplifies the complex, time-consuming, and error-prone nature of releasing new software into production. While Google's contribution to cloud-native automation is groundbreaking, its practice of building ecosystems is what makes Kubernetes so compelling. Instead of attempting to control and own the entire landscape of Kubernetes's capabilities, Google has invited others with complementary expertise to help develop, enhance, and expand the core offering.

For example, Apprenda, a well-regarded enterprise cloud tooling company, provides modern cloud development infrastructure that is designed to help developers radically accelerate both software development and deployment to the cloud. It turns out that Apprenda spent several years building extensive expertise in automation infrastructure designed to integrate with and support the Microsoft development community. As Google's Kubernetes framework expanded in functionality, marketplace interest in leveraging Kubernetes in the Microsoft developer community increased. Apprenda saw this opportunity and approached Google with an offer to lead an effort in building out the Kubernetes capabilities related to the Microsoft tooling landscape. Not only did Google respond positively, but it also extended every possible resource to support Apprenda in this role.

This new, vibrant expansion of the Kubernetes ecosystem has enabled Google to enjoy a competitive advantage as it more rapidly expands coverage into the Microsoft community. Similarly, Apprenda now enjoys being the developer automation infrastructure of choice. Most importantly, both companies are now innovating faster than they could have had they remained singularly invested in the winner-takes-all view of their markets. This illustrates the ability of digital ecosystems to drive technical and business model innovation.

In *The Martian*, when Mark Watney set out to survive Mars, he envisioned his future back on Earth, constantly looking to his existing resources to see new ways forward. If you intend to deliver digital, you must follow suit, starting where you are and following yes, looking both immediately ahead and further into the future for ever-evolving opportunities. By continuously reimagining the future and by recognizing the shifts happening in your company and the market ecosystem, you can surge to the next wave — and the next.

Now, it's time to begin your Digital Wave journey.

Chapter 2

The Digital Wave Journey

Capital One was formed in the late 1980s as a division of Bank of Virginia and was taken public in 1994. The original leaders, Rich Fairbank and Nigel Morris, established the company on both technical *and* business agility. Fairbank and Morris recognized that credit cards were more about information than banking. Card products that banks offered in those days conformed to the early mindset of Henry Ford: Any customer can have a car painted any color that he wants so long as it is black, but from the beginning Capital One applied an innovative design to its enterprise structure and its technology.

Business agility was *built in* so that "low-cost information processing would enable them to create a new kind of company, [one] that operated like a scientific laboratory for mass customization . . . Through constant testing of direct-marketing offers, the company could evolve the right product to deliver to the right customer at the right time and at the right price, for many different sets of customers." [1] Technical agility was based on a "proprietary set of information systems . . . conduct[ing] dozens of experiments each day . . . allowing [Capital One] to experiment with different real-time responses to ad offers."[2] Capital One differentiated itself by taking advantage of its technical ability to make sense of and manage the vast amount of data this produced. A worthy mission with a huge financial upside.

Capital One's business model personalizes products and services (in most cases a credit card or financial service) based on a customer's unique credit risk and revenue profile. Though widely accepted today, in 1987 no one thought it was possible to pursue one-to-one marketing and continuous customization of offers. [3] Card products were competing on the 1989 innovation by Citibank and American Airlines, offering reward points for using their cards.

Capital One's first big breakthrough, balance transfer offers (so common today that it is hard to imagine this as an innovation), used their business model to transform the industry. Following the recession of 1982-83, consumers had increased their spending and, aided by the end of usury laws and inflation, profitability for banks soared. As competition in the credit card industry increased, banks targeted users who were the most lucrative to

---

1 John Henry Clippinger, III, ed., *Biology of Business: Decoding the Natural Laws of Enterprise*, Jossey-Bass Business & Management (San Francisco: Jossey-Bass, 1999), 141–152.

2 Ibid.

3 Rakesh Kumar Sharma et al., "Customer Relationship management at Capital One (UK) (Condensed Version)," authorSTREAM, accessed May 18, 2017, http://www.authorstream.com/Presentation/rakesh208-709520-customer-relationship-management-capital-one-uk/.

them: those who carried a balance from month to month. Capital One used its information systems and in-market experimentation algorithms to identify customers who carried *no balance* and offered them a low 'teaser' rate when they consolidated all their cards into one credit card, turning them into more profitable accounts.

The success of this experiment established the Capital One test and learn strategy.[4] This customer-focused, product-based approach measures the costs and revenues associated with each offer that is tested in the marketplace. At the time, Capital One actually *expected* 99 percent of the offers tested to fail,[5] but the small percentage that would succeed were—and are—well suited for the fast-paced, volatile credit card and financial markets, which, while uncertain, have huge upside potential. At Capital One the freedom to fail is built into its corporate culture, and it is this freedom that has created the conditions for the company's greatest innovations!

Still, Capital One's novel approach to product offerings would not have been possible if not for the visionary software architecture used at the time: The founders saw IT not as a way to automate, but as a way to innovate. By building systems using reusable components, Capital One enjoyed an enormous speed advantage, and it prototyped new product capabilities that competitors couldn't match (and recall, this was 30 years ago). This advantage helped them to achieve their early corporate goal of making sure that 80 percent of Capital One's portfolio was consistently less than two years old.

---

4 Charles Fishman, "This Is a Marketing Revolution," *Fast Company*, April 30, 1999, https://www.fastcompany.com/36975/marketing-revolution.

5 John Henry Clippinger, III, ed., op. cit.

How did they maintain this rate of adaptive and technological change? By operating with less structure, less hierarchy, and less bureaucracy. Marketers, analysts, and IT functioned as loosely coupled units and focused on experimenting with customers, using direct marketing techniques. Some teams were tasked with identifying and growing new lines of business, and in the first four years they generated 80 new business concepts—most of which failed. Still, what they learned propelled them forward.

The example of Capital One points out that a relatively mature, highly regulated industry can exploit the same principles you see at work in today's most powerful digital natives—Amazon, Netflix, and Google. More importantly, Capital One illustrates that digital transformation and agility are not things you acquire off the shelf; they are part of a continuous journey of experimentation, disruption, and transformation.

Let's look at another example of digital transformation. ING Netherlands recently decided to give enormous autonomy and responsibility to small product squads, relinquishing its traditional hierarchy. According to Mary Poppendieck's eye-opening case study, "The End of Enterprise IT," after initial IT-based experiments, the ING Netherlands leadership team had "examined its business model and come to an interesting conclusion: Their bank was no longer a financial services company, it was a technology company in the financial services business."[6] That conclusion drove ING Netherlands into an astounding journey of digital transformation.

ING realized something that every company navigating an authentic digital transformation grasps sooner or later: Digital transformation is a transformation of the entire organization, not just IT.

---

6 *The Lean Mindset* (blog), January 14, 2017, http://www.leanessays.com/2017/01 the-end-of-enterprise-it.html.

As Poppendieck put it, "If you are going through an agile transformation in your IT department, you are thinking too narrowly. Digitization must be an organization-wide experience."[7]

So what does it actually mean to transform to digital? Perhaps it is amassing huge amounts of data (i.e., Big Data). Or maybe it's a platform that uses algorithms and predictive analytics to gain insights into this data. Or perhaps it's the organizational culture, teaming methods (e.g., Scrum and Kanban) and software automation (e.g., DevOps and the cloud) that allow your employees to operate with hyperagility. Actually, we think it is all these, combined and made available to employees as a digital fabric that is always on, always available, and infinitely composable, enabling existing teams and technology to evolve into new structures that can be reconfigured endlessly to match market challenges with little friction, effort, and time.

THE DIGITAL WAVE MODEL: AN OVERVIEW

The Digital Wave Model (Figure 2.1) illustrates how waves of technical and organizational transformation occur simultaneously and depicts the technical and organizational traits that companies operating within each wave share.

Wave 0 represents companies whose corporate structure, culture, and operating principles reflect the attitude that digital and IT are merely tools for cost reduction and process automation. Wave 0 companies are risk averse and believe they should pursue digital initiatives only with significant upfront planning, and then only after both risk mitigation and return on investment are clear. These companies typically operate with a style of project development frequently referred to as "waterfall." They are focused on efficiency

---

7 Ibid.

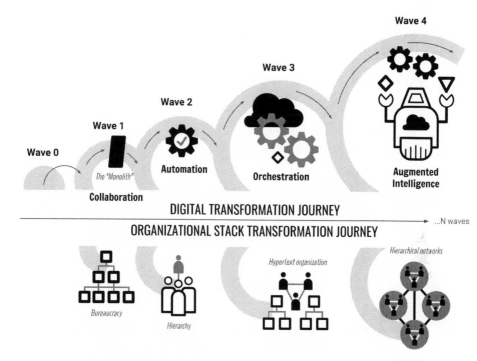

Figure 2.1. **Digital Wave Model. Waves of technical transformation require the organization to change structure and function in order to survive and advance.**

and are functionally centralized, with discrete business silos. Their view of the market is inside-out, i.e., customers receiving what they deliver and providing feedback after the fact.

Wave 1 emerged in the late 1990s as tech-savvy start-ups began to codify and promote a new set of iterative, more collaborative organizing and execution methods for building digital products and services. In 2001 the Agile Manifesto was published and gave way to a movement that promoted a self-described agile value system, along with guiding principles on which companies could more successfully envision, build, and deploy software systems. Today, the agile movement has progressed from fringe to mainstream. Nearly every large company is now attempting to establish agile methods as a replacement for the more common waterfall style of project management.

Between 2007 and 2015, lean manufacturing principles were also applied to software development. This provided legacy technology companies another set of tools for gaining efficiencies[8] using an economically viable product development process[9], and incorporating customer feedback early and often.[10] By 2015 lean and agile practices had combined to establish an enterprise-wide perspective[11] that gave traditional companies a doorway into the technologies of Wave 2 and beyond. For these companies digital was no longer just a tech play — it became a business play.

However, many traditional companies believed that Wave 1 was the digital destination. These companies optimized for this waypoint with a variety of scaling frameworks designed to enable IT to benefit from greater efficiencies — technical transformation — without having to undergo the pain of business and organizational transformation. This brings us to the challenges — and advantages — of moving from Wave 1 to Wave 2.

Wave 2 is where many of the digital brands began and live, particularly those most admired by consumers. This wave begins by advancing use of cloud and automation infrastructures, radically accelerating the work IT specialists previously performed. The wave

8 Mary and Tom Poppendieck, *Implementing Lean Software Development: From Concept to Cash*, Pearson Education, Inc., Boston, MA, 2007.

9 Donald Reinertsen, *The Principles of Product Development Flow: Second Generation Lean Product Development*, Celeritas Publishing, Redondo Beach, CA, 2009.

10 Eric Ries, *The Lean Startup: How Today's Entrepreneurs Use Continuous Innovation to Create Radically Successful Businesses*, Crown Business, New York, NY, 2011.

11 Jez Humble, Joanne Molesky and Barry O'Reilly, *Lean Enterprise: How High Performing Organizations Innovate at Scale*, O'Reilly Media, Inc., Sebastopol, CA, 2015.

of automation, while dramatically speeding up the execution of digital product development, injects tension into the organization. To navigate successfully to Wave 2, organizations must drastically reduce their reliance on bureaucracy, command-and-control management, departmental silos, centralized planning, and traditional project and change management.

Wave 2 disrupts the authority and decision-making of the org chart, shifting them to specific roles (product owners), people (subject matter experts), and structures (end-to-end feature teams). This challenges the bureaucratic assumption that leaders at the top have the requisite knowledge and expertise to make good and timely decisions, and opens the way for a healthy hierarchy to emerge. Distributing authority and decision-making to what we call the working surface — literally where work gets done — produces *better* choices, *faster* feedback, and *cheaper* business outcomes . . . the old mantra delivered in a completely different way!

As companies adopt Wave 2 technologies and organizing principles, new opportunities, markets, and ways of creating value appear. Wave 2 companies build on self-managing teams by introducing self-governance, establishing autonomous, end-to-end product development teams. Self-governance supports vertical and horizontal alignment to corporate goals, encourages the use of leading indicators (vs. lagging), and enables radical alteration of the way the organization is structured in terms of operating and human systems — preparing the company for adopting the patterns and technology of Wave 3.

Wave 3 is where the elite digital natives currently live. These companies give birth to entirely new market ecosystems that require even more dramatic corporate transformation. Wave 3 companies toggle between operating as a hierarchy and operating as a network. Formalized networks spring up as the means for innovation, solutions to problems and dependencies, and the fastest way to incorporate real-time operations and customer data into business offerings; while hierarchy remains the structure for strategic direction, personnel and career development, and routine work performed most efficiently at scale.

Within and across ecosystems, Wave 3 companies add self-organization to self-management and self-governance. From the Wave 0 perspective, these three attributes of the new corporate management system amount to loss of control. To be sure, Wave 3 requires the loss of *command-and-control*, but using self-management, self-governance, and self-organization empowers all parts of the company to safely thrive at "the edge of chaos."

Wave 3 companies also nurture digital platforms that are explicitly designed to include and rely upon an ecosystem of partners and third-party complementors, which include both companies and consumers. In this brave new world, Wave 3 companies are intentionally inviting others to contribute to—even to lead—certain aspects of strategy and innovation within their platform ecosystem. This moves them from a winner-takes-all model to a cooperative ecosystem, the net effect being greater innovation.[12] Platforms in Wave 3 integrate business, sales, and marketing folks into tech-savvy communities, often operating on the platforms of others, to generate business ideas that were unimaginable in the previous waves. These ecosystems prepare the way for future waves of technology and transformation.

Wave 4 is just now emerging, so the story is being written as we go to press. In general, Wave 4 is the wave of cognitive computing as technical systems become more self-aware and intelligent. Algorithms will increasingly do the work of employees, and artificial

---

12 Sangeet Paul Choudary, *Platform Scale: How an engorging business model helps startups build large empires with minimum investment.* Platform Thinking Labs, 2015.

intelligence will progressively take on the work of many professionals. Though it is almost invisible to the non-tech world, this wave is already affecting companies and consumers. A great example of this vision is Corning Glass. Watch their video, *A Day Made of Glass (https://www.youtube.com/watch?v=X-GXO_urMow)*, to see the future.

Waves 5, 6, 7? . . . Did we mention that there is no end in sight?

SAILING TO THE HORIZON: THE WAVE 3 COMPANY

Wave 3 is the horizon that, we believe, a company must prioritize from the moment it leaves Wave 0 — so as not to get stuck in Waves 1 and 2 (Figure 2.2). Companies in Wave 3 are no longer top-down bureaucracies; they are both a hierarchy and a network operating in a fabric of real-time data. Because few traditional companies have made the transformation all the way from Wave 0 to Wave 3, we understand it best by observing today's leading digital native companies.

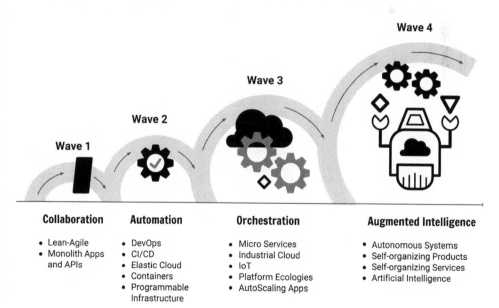

Figure 2.2 **The technology stack across the digital waves.**

Wave 3 technology relies on orchestration,[13] which is the outcome of Wave 2 automation and continuous integration and delivery efforts, and which enables microservices and scalable business
operations. From a systems-thinking perspective, Wave 3 orchestration is holistic: All teams understand how their part integrates into
a systemic whole, and they intentionally contribute to optimize the
whole. From a resource perspective, this means that some teams
and products may be sub-optimized for the greater good of the
company, which dramatically changes internal politics and power.

By breaking down monoliths into microservices, Wave 3 companies organize themselves in novel ways, such as microbusinesses.
Microbusinesses experiment in their markets by combining existing
products and services into higher-order, composite offerings and testing them in the marketplace. Those that successfully fulfill a customer
need can stabilize on that need, building a platform and/or ecosystem.

That is the technical side of orchestration. The human side
orchestrates relationships and cooperative commitments on platforms and in ecosystems.[14] This generates a *hypertext organization*, which

---

13 Cripe, Billy, "What Is Business Alignment?" Quora, November 24, 2015,
    https://www.quora.com/What-is-business-alignment; Hewlett Packard
    Enterprise, "Operations Orchestration," accessed May 18, 2017 http://www8.
    hp.com/us/en/software-solutions/operations-orchestration-it-process-
    automation/; MuleSoft, "What Is Application Orchestration?" accessed May
    18, 2017, https://www.mulesoft.com/resources/esb/what-application-
    orchestration.

14 Deloitte research that sorts companies into four broad categories based on
    their chief economic activity: asset builders, service providers, technology
    creators, and network orchestrators. Barry Libert, Yoram (Jerry) Wind, and
    Megan Beck, "What Airbnb, Uber, and Alibaba Have in Common," *Harvard
    Business Review*, November 20, 2014, https://hbr.org/2014/11/what-airbnb-uber-
    and-alibaba-have-in-common?webSyncID=32cb45e0-2a2c-8c3d-0a20-
    6683a9b237b1&sessionGUID=4ae5d58e-2682-ade9-ceac-ae9ac7c6351c.

we have adapted from the work of Nonaka and Takeuchi.[15] A hypertext organizational design emphasizes both hierarchy and networks, using the two to be both stable (hierarchical) and dynamic (networked). The enterprise as a whole is stable while the parts are in constant motion, a system balanced at the edge of chaos as information and resources flow through the company.

At any point in time, a part of the company, business unit, or value stream may be operating in one state or the other. Performance management, finance and budgeting, and regulatory/compliance activities usually fall within the hierarchical structure. Innovation, product development, and removal of dependencies or bottlenecks are activities best addressed by the network structure, which is capable of spanning boundaries and functions. Utilizing both, bureaucracy is replaced by a high-level hierarchy, which reveals progressively finer-grained networks of autonomy and value creation.

As in the cases of Capital One and ING Netherlands, Wave 3 thrives in a culture that embraces risk and experimentation. The organizational structure and leadership are distributed, increasing the speed of decision-making and idea validation. Distributed structures place people with diverse expertise into cross-functional teams that have everything they need to take an idea and turn it into a concrete offering, end-to-end, one that can be tested and released into the market.

In Wave 3, access to resources (information, tools, people, and platforms) outweighs ownership, which dramatically shifts the levers of control. The increased exposure to users (customers) and complementors (platform and ecosystem members) creates a sense-and-respond interaction with the market. This makes the distributed ecosystem

---

15 Ikujiro Nonaka and Hirotaka Takeuchi, *The Knowledge-Creating Company: How Japanese Companies Create the Dynamics of Innovation.* Oxford University Press, New York, NY, 1995.

structure more innovative and the companies that use it more robust.

Further, Wave 3 generates a third technical manifesto — the Reactive Manifesto[16] — which emphasizes responsiveness, resiliency, elasticity, and asynchronous message-passing (as delineated in the insert below). These technical requirements further the need for organizational and operational transformation. While Wave 3 is a giant step into the unknown for most enterprises and may feel uncomfortable — at times even downright scary — it is essential for navigating the waves to come.

The Digital Wave Model helps us explore not just how new technologies — such as programmable infrastructure, the cloud, and microservices — can be exploited, but also how the organizing

---

THE REACTIVE MANIFESTO

RESPONSIVE: Problems are detected quickly and dealt with effectively. Response times are rapid and reliable, and deliver a consistent quality of service.

RESILIENT: Robustness is achieved by replication, containment, isolation, and delegation. System breakdowns are contained within each component, ensuring that parts of the system can fail without compromising the whole.

ELASTIC: Ability to react to changes in inputs is achieved by increasing or decreasing the resources allocated to service these inputs.

MESSAGE-DRIVEN: Asynchronous message-passing establishes an asymmetrical, flexible boundary between components.

---

16 Jonas Bonér et al., "The Reactive Manifesto," September 16, 2014, www.reactivemanifesto.org.; https://www.lightbend.com/blog/reactive-manifesto-20

principles and structures of organizations must be reshaped or tuned to exploit each new technical stack.

Your company may very well make the needed investments in technical advances, but the digital products and services you conceive, build, and deploy can be constrained by your organizational structure and culture. Put differently, without technological *and* organizational transformation working together, your company risks designing, building, and deploying uninspired stuff, all with bleeding-edge, cloud-native technology. This is *not* a strategy for advancing through the waves; rather, it is a strategy for being marginalized by customers who move on to enjoy the products of more evolved competitors.

How to make this continuous journey of technological and organizational transformation is what we endeavor to cover from this point forward. For some, the ideas, methods, challenges, and opportunities presented here may induce vertigo. For others, there will be joy and celebration. For many, there will be denial, disbelief, and a wait-and-see attitude — it is these who rest in the most dangerous place.

PRINCIPLES OF DIGITAL DISRUPTION

For all companies today, there are three principles driving digital disruption that cannot be ignored. Regardless of your starting point, your company's transformation journey must contend with the following truths:

Digital Principle #1:
There Will Always Be a New Wave Headed Your Way

Surge focuses on the first four waves (Wave 0 through Wave 3) because we have the clarity to make sense of them and enough information to make recommendations about them. And we urge you to view Wave 3 as the first horizon, a port where you can safely drop anchor.

This horizon positions you to navigate the emerging waves, Wave 4 and beyond.

The most immediate danger you face is getting stuck in Wave 1.

Hundreds, if not thousands, of blogs and pitches are written for companies sitting in Wave 0 or hunkered down in Wave 1. The gist: "All you need is our tool, technology, coaches, or consultants, and you are all set. Sign here and we will start tomorrow." These pitches are typically made to IT, and IT almost never partners with corporate leaders or enrolls their business partners when saying yes. This disconnect is the most common cause of what we call *the clay layer* between IT and the rest of the corporation. The clay layer signifies a barrier: The flow of information, which should move in both directions, becomes clogged.

The most dangerous, if most appealing, part of the above-mentioned pitches is their certainty; their writers claim to know the destination, and they say that they can take you there. Digital Principle #1 debunks this myth, acknowledging that *there is* no destination . . . and there may not be one for decades, for the advances in digital technology are only in their early stages. They are currently akin to what factories were when they were using cheap labor during the Industrial Age. Transformational movements such as Toyota Production Systems and lean manufacturing wouldn't reach their prime until a century after their inception. Even taking into account the accelerated rate of development in the digital age, the digital waves are just beginning to form.

Digital Principle #2:
You Must Acquire New and Abandon Old

Let us introduce you to a word not often used these days: *jettison*. It dates from the mid-nineteenth century, when jettisoning meant throwing things overboard *to lighten and balance the load* on a ship. During an emergency or in turbulent situations, *moving crafts* (e.g., ships, air-craft, and spacecraft) use jettisoning to stabilize themselves.

On this digital journey, your company can be seen as a moving craft. You are in motion, and you are likely to be unstable at times. Before you decide what you are going to acquire, you need to deter-mine what must be left behind to maintain momentum and bal-ance. For example, if you have decided to adopt agile teams, DevOps automation, and/or cloud-native application development tools, you must confront and navigate the challenge of leaving behind, say, command-and-control management, burdensome HR practices, and central planning.

Deciding what to acquire and what to abandon has implications both locally — at the business and functional unit level — and at the corporate level. A global or large regional enterprise can-not — repeat, cannot — traverse the waves as a single, tightly cou-pled unit. Some parts of the organization will naturally race ahead while others will lag behind. Some parts may need to get to Wave 3 quickly, yet other parts might stay comfortably at Wave 1 for a time.

In this climate a universal command or tooling decree does not work. Teams, businesses, and functions have to do the hard work of figuring out what they need and what they will give up. Execu-tives have the task of enabling a heterogeneous ecosystem to emerge from a homogeneous corporation.

Digital Principle #3:
Both Human and Technical Dimensions Drive Transformation

Humans are social. Our brains are wired to connect with one another. Our human communities (i.e., our networks), combined with our emotions, *positively* inform our decisions. In addition, our unconscious mind influences the beliefs and biases of our worldview, our relationships, and, by definition, our actions. What takes place in our unconscious is often strictly unavailable to our conscious minds, though we very often witness the effects of these unconscious beliefs and biases. Your colleagues can save you time and time again on the digital journey, but you have to let them be the creative, emotional, and autonomous humans they are.

The other dimension, technology, is the fuel of the digital fire . . . and it is burning hot and fast. What will slow you down in your technical transformation will not be learning how to use it, or even finding people who want to implement the latest technical widget and shiny new object; it will be transforming the organizational structure to metabolize all this new capacity and capability.

The Greek word *tekhne*, from which we draw our word *technology*, means art or craft, often in relation to craftsmanship; and the word *tekhnologia* refers to a systematic treatment. Using this etymology, if we were to define *technology* more broadly, as a systematic treatment of practical craftsmanship, then organizational design is the technology you need now. The practical craft needed for product development and digital organizational design comes from complexity and systems theory, from psychology and neurobiology, and from ecology and anthropology. In other words, traditional management and business practices are not going to help you right now. They need to be rewritten *while* your company makes this journey.

ACTIVATING THE NETWORK WITHIN THE HIERARCHY

During the Industrial Age the design and implementation of corporate structure was enacted using paper and pencil. This was possible because industrial organizational design was based on the limited actions of the individual worker — typically *repeatable*, highly *prescribed*, and easily *visible* to the manager. Because of the slow and predictable market evolution, conditions were favorable for vertical control of work activities and tightly coupled processes that governed workers' actions. This produced an effective hierarchy, without a lot of bureaucracy.

Back then, according to Frederick Taylor's *Scientific Management*, process controlled individuals, producing conformity and efficiency at the individual level. To coordinate and control factories and assembly lines, a hierarchy of managers allowed a single individual to control the behaviors of many workers. Corporate hierarchy became an established organizing principle through which a manager or executive could "manage" the collective behavior of large parts of the company without directing the behavior of any single individual.

As technology advanced, the complexity of products and the collective behavior of workers increased; so did interdependencies, interactions, and unintended consequences. As a result, the span of control for any single manager necessarily contracted. This increased the ranks of management, and the simple hierarchy quickly became a complicated bureaucracy. It is easy to see that in such a scenario control is necessarily achieved and maintained at the expense of corporate agility and market responsiveness.

Add to this the complexity of high-tech knowledge work, and the span of control for managers dramatically diminishes. This leaves managers unable to make sound decisions quickly, especially when they need information and approval from other parts of the company. Accordingly, the whole workflow system slows. Physically, intellectually, and emotionally, managers no longer have the bandwidth to maintain the pace required of them. The result? Companies suddenly require more and more managers for smaller, more specialized teams. And over time bureaucratic bloat and process rigidity take over.

In most corporations, middle managers are everywhere, and standardized processes rule every decision and action. Teams require multiple tools and meetings to coordinate small acts of value creation. Even though you have SharePoint, Slack, a team wiki page, multiple project management tools, and a prioritized product backlog, it seems you can't get work done quickly. Conditions continue to deteriorate as you attempt to move across the technical waves. The company's organizational structure is a monolith, and you are struggling to incorporate agile teams, lean workflow, and advanced technology into it.

Those who have operated in a bureaucratic corporate structure, either as a manager or as an employee, know how poorly it works. When knowledge work and digital technology are the context for creating value, the organizational structure must function and thrive using agility, creatively reacting to rapid, unpredictable change, and operating at the edge of chaos. To become a digital powerhouse — or even digital capable — companies must redesign themselves from an industrial-age assembly line to become a knowledge-creating human ecosystem.

This means that moving from Wave 0 to Wave 3, requires creating an organization capable of (1) coordinating large numbers of diverse, specialized teams (and individuals); (2) providing fast, visible information that produces alignment, avoids collisions (unintended consequences and negative impacts), and generates local cohesion[17]; while (3) matching the complexity of the market ecosystem with the complexity of your corporate behaviors — in short, a stable yet highly dynamic organizational design. These conditions allow us to toggle between the stable hierarchy and dynamic network of the hypertext organization.

We find stable yet dynamic structures in nature where there is flow.

---

17 Reynolds, Craig, "Boids: Background and Update," September 6, 2001, http://www.red3d.com/cwr/boids/.

Flow, in the way we are using it, shapes the medium through which it moves, most obvious in river beds created by water currents, but also evident in movement of information and ideas through organizations.[18] Flow of information and ideas through companies establishes the shape and functionality of collaboration, networks, and culture. It generates the evolution of organizational design—important as companies move through the technical waves, creating superior, more frictionless flows of innovation.

This is important because, when speed of change or complexity of the information in the market ecosystem exceeds the ability of the organization to stream the information across the company, the organization becomes unstable.[19] It is easy to see that the technical and market complexity of Wave 2 (automation) and Wave 3 (orchestration) far exceeds the ability of traditional bureaucracies to communicate and disperse information across the company. Bureaucracy—that is, excessive process and rigid hierarchy—limits people's ability to respond to challenges with multiple diverse actions, patterns, and/or behaviors. The only patterns available under such a system are top-down, command-and-control, and up-and-over, and in this structure, autonomy, self-organization, complex coordination, and responsiveness are sacrificed.

But there is a fairly simple, yet completely viable and successful, solution: Instead of struggling to maintain a bureaucracy for

18 Adrian Bejan and J. Peder Zane, *Design in Nature: How the Constructal Law Governs Evolution in Biology, Physics, Technology, and Social Organizations*. Doubleday, New York, NY, 2012.

19 Yaneer Bar-Yam, *Complexity Rising: From Human Beings to Human Civilization, a Complexity Profile*, (Cambridge, MA: New England Complex Systems Institute, December 1997).

coordination and control, we can use the natural social physics of humans to achieve digital transformation by incorporating network structures into our organizational hierarchies. This is why gutting the middle of your company is unnecessary. In fact, it is the wrong action. Instead, you can use those middle managers strategically to establish horizontal networks. To remove bureaucracy, turn the middle into a horizontal network (see Chapter 8) and use them to flow work, information, and ideas in all directions. Empower the middle to create dynamic, stable, and frictionless flows of innovative products, services, and ideas.

Understanding this provides us the means for making the journey from corporate monolith to networked microbusinesses (Figure 2.3).

We see the transformation from bureaucracy to network ecosystems as the means of producing coordinated, complex, collective behavior, which is the advantage enjoyed by digital natives like Amazon, Google, and Netflix. They have forged their organizations

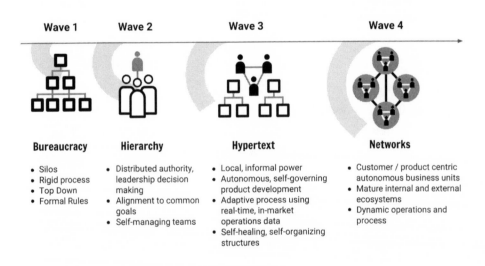

Figure 2.3. **Organizational charts depicting bureaucracy, hierarchy, hypertext, and network operating models.**

in the fire of digital complexity, facing challenges that they could meet only by using nontraditional means. Following Conway's Law[20] they built their companies to reflect the structure of the software they produce. This enables their companies to be highly competitive in fast-paced, dynamic market ecosystems. It does not mean we need to jettison hierarchy altogether; hierarchy is a form of network. Rather, we need to jettison bureaucracy and adopt organizational structures that use both hierarchy and networks to accommodate the complexity of today's markets and technologies.

Ultimately, the role of corporate leaders in the digital wave journey is to transform their people, processes, and structures from a bureaucracy to loosely coupled networks and from vertical silos to a highly connected web. Part of this effort requires a shift from projects to products; however, the biggest shifts are in organizational design and business model innovation (i.e., from business units to microbusinesses). These require leaders to transform their mindsets, means of coordination and control, and daily activities (Chapter 9).

As companies move through the waves, the need for real-time coordination and collaboration increases exponentially. And so does the need for flexibility, decentralization, speed, and accurate information flow — all of which are critical for establishing platforms that promote access, multisided markets, and interdependent communities. This produces a world absent of the familiar habits and structures of traditional management that simply no longer work. Now we need to explore what replaces these.

---

20 Mel Conway, http://www.melconway.com/Home/Conways_Law.html

Chapter 3

Control without Bureaucracy

In the early 2000s it wasn't uncommon to visit someone's house and see a red Netflix envelope on the DVD player or kitchen counter. The slim paper envelopes were a revolution. For many of us, gone were the days of due dates, late fees, and driving to the video store.

If you were a Netflix customer, you probably remember the careful grooming of your Netflix queue, the quick watch-and-send-back you'd do if you *really* wanted to get through a television season, and even the frustration of not getting the next video on your list because it was rented out. Netflix had its users wrapped around its entertainment-providing finger. As Starbucks changed the customer experience of coffee shops, Netflix altered the experience of home entertainment.

Yet despite the genius behind the concept, becoming an entertainment gamechanger was neither the main idea nor a simple process for Netflix. Disrupting the entire content distribution industry required continuous transformation and multiple corporate discontinuities.

The founders, Reed Hastings and Marc Randolph, built a company that embraced a culture of risk tolerance, nurtured innovation, and operated in the sweet spot at the edge of chaos.

Hastings and Randolph met and were commuting buddies while working for Pure Atria, a software company. When the company was acquired by Rational Software, they were both out of a job and began to explore what they could do next.[1] When they heard about the new video format, DVD, that was going to be sold like records, it triggered the idea that they could replace unwieldy VHS tapes with an e-commerce movie rental business model. To test their idea they bought used CDs, put them in greeting card envelopes, and mailed them to Hastings' house. As Hastings explained to *Fortune* magazine, "It was a long twenty-four hours until the mail arrived back at my house, and I ripped them open and they were all in great shape. That was the big excitement point."[2]

Netflix started out as an alternative to Blockbuster — movies sold or rented through the mail — at this point still physical assets rather than digital assets. But early on they confronted the fact that they needed a new business model to survive. Faced with the fact that selling DVDs (97 percent of their early revenue came from sales) would be challenged by every mass market retailer, they decided to change their business model to movie rental only. Randolph, a consumer market expert, describes their thinking: "'We can either keep on muddling along and have a reasonable success, or we can bet everything on the long shot. But if we hit it, we'll be in a much, much better position. We'll be uniquely

---

1 https://www.bizjournals.com/sanjose/news/2014/01/08/netflixs-first-ceo-on-reed-hastings.html

2 http://archive.fortune.com/2009/01/27/news/newsmakers/hastings_netflix.fortune/index.htm

differentiated.' And we did that. We dropped the sales and bet it all on rental." [3]

Netflix kicked off their new rental strategy by partnering with Amazon, a pattern that they would repeat over and over to support their fledgling business. The deal they struck was: If Amazon would promote their DVD rentals on Amazon.com, Netflix would stop selling them (even though this decision had already been made!). This avoided head-to-head competition, strengthened the nascent DVD market, and gave both companies a new audience. The Amazon partnership offset the initial loss of sales that Netflix experienced, and they gained huge amounts of free advertising—along with a new focus. Reynolds summarized it this way, "Believe me, that tends to focus the mind when you walk away from 97 percent of your revenue . . . part of the Netflix DNA—which is this deep sense of focus, this sense of testing, the sense of being metrically driven—comes from those early days." [4]

Similar to Blockbuster's, the initial Netflix business model was not subscription based. "I remember thinking, 'God, this whole thing could go down'," Hastings told *Fortune*, "and we said, 'Let's try the more radical subscription idea.' We knew it wouldn't be terrible, but we didn't know if it would be great." [5] Subscription movie rentals, a questionably progressive idea at the time, was born from the recognition that Netflix was *too much* like Blockbuster. Not certain of the outcome, or the journey it would create, Netflix nonetheless launched a free subscription trial in late 1999. Within a month 80

3 https://www.bizjournals.com/sanjose/news/2014/01/08/netflixs-first-ceo-on-reed-hastings.html

4 Ibid.

5 http://archive.fortune.com/2009/01/27/news/newsmakers/hastings_netflix.fortune/index.htm

percent of the trial users had converted to the paid subscriptions. In response to this successful experiment, Netflix again transformed their business model.

Yet having unlimited due dates and no late fees remained a huge risk. Would customers use online queues? Remember, this was the world of dial-up modems and VHS; very few early adopters used DVDs, and DVD players were rare and expensive. VHS players, on the other hand, were ubiquitous, cheap, and supported by Blockbuster. Hastings began engaging big DVD players like Toshiba, HP, and Apple, in a repeat of the Amazon partnership strategy. He positioned Netflix as a niche complementor, one that his ecosystem partners could use to their benefit. Netflix, with their list of subscribers, supported the fledgling DVD industry, and Hastings built a relational network in which his partners offered free Netflix DVD rentals with the purchase of their DVD players.

For the time being, Hastings had solved the problem the emerging DVD platform posed, and Netflix spread across the DVD ecosystem. But they weren't done. The company next used this strategy to establish revenue-sharing agreements with film and television production companies, negotiate sole distribution rights with several independent film producers, and promote aspiring filmmakers. These mutually enhancing relationships strengthened and broadened their ecosystem, allowing Netflix to experiment and learn production, and continued to transform and grow the company and the market.

Hastings and Randolph did not start Netflix with the vision of streaming video (although there was talk of digital movies in 1997) or producing movies. Rather, Netflix learned its way forward, disruption by disruption and innovation by innovation. This they continue today. In each self-imposed disruptive space, companies like Netflix find transformational ideas that propel them forward. They are constantly operating on the verge of disorder, the edge of chaos, but transforming on purpose and with intention, to keep themselves moving.

Today's top-down management practices stop less forward-thinking companies from transforming the way Netflix does. Such practices keep companies from engaging fully with the digital tsunami. It's easy to see why: Top-down management practices were invented during the Industrial Revolution, an era left behind when we entered the information age. Yet information age management paradigms have done little more than embroider upon the command-and-control structures they inherited. If we're going to reinvent companies to traverse continuous, disruptive digital waves, we need a completely new way of managing organizational life. We need a revolution in the way companies navigate, adjust to, and prosper from digital change, and it has to start with a reinvention of management itself.

Shocked? Probably not. The managers and employees we work with tell us stories about the daily frustrations that arise from the (often unintentional) conflict between top-down management control and bottom-up market dynamics. Top-down controls can't cope with the speed and dynamic range of changes now washing over companies. It's time for a candid and honest acknowledgment: We need an alternative management system for a world gone digital.

THE DIGITAL MANAGEMENT CRISIS

Today industries and markets move at speeds measured in weeks and months, not years. Any company hoping to thrive in this new world must commit to a radical reinvention of management, including moving from centralized control to network-based self-organization. Yet the very idea of organizational structures designed to enable large-scale autonomy and self-organizing behavior is foreign to most corporate leaders. The corporate designers who launched today's global enterprises sought to build the perfect machine, but, as we've seen, our management systems were never designed to handle continuously changing, highly connected, interdependent markets, let alone ecosystems that invite others (including competitors) to create products on our "proprietary" platforms.

Welcome to the digital age.

Digital requires seeing the company as composed of humans — humans who in large social groups operate as complex adaptive systems. Complex adaptive systems are alive, and within them interactions constantly change, people learn, and the environment evolves. These systems naturally generate novelty because their components interact with each other in *unpredictable* ways in response to changes in their environment and based on rich feedback networks. This makes corporations less like machines and much more like the humans that compose them. Yet many leaders today still persist in designing corporations like machines.

The difference between a complex adaptive system and a complicated machine is this: Of the two, only a complex adaptive system can *routinely spawn innovations that arise from the interactions and interdependencies among the parts.*

Of course these two systems cannot be entirely separated from one another. Today complicated machine-like systems and complex adaptive systems are both at play in corporations. In fact, they are intertwined. The challenge for management is to find ways to blend these two worlds and use both to create value and enable rapid, often radical, change. The struggle is to know what to control and what to set free.

Let's examine the Digital Wave Model from the perspective of the organizational transformation that must take place to support technology. To evolve your technology you must move away from bureaucracy and, with each new wave, transform your organization.

This is possible *only because* your company is a complex adaptive system and not a machine.

In Waves 0 and 1 bureaucracy defines the corporate structure, operating model, and environment (culture, norms, leadership, etc.). Most large companies have at their core the bureaucratic, centralized planning services and controls that govern the company's every decision, action, and investment. Information, resources, and commands radiate from the core to the outer parts of the organization, determining the actions and behaviors of others. Authority and decision-making are tightly coupled to the org chart, reinforced by formal roles and rules (such as standards and prescriptive processes). The result is conformity: People do as they are told—or often even wait to do anything *until* they are told!

The danger here, as digital markets grow to predominate, is that the most critical market interactions—those actively connecting companies with customers and competitors—operate at the edge of the company, the base of the organizational pyramid, which has the most direct knowledge of the marketplace. These peripheral sensors channel new information to the top for processing thousands of times a day. Management's role is to interpret the information as it moves up and down the hierarchy, ultimately providing feedback to the edge in the form of decisions and directives. In the conventional corporate structure, people who typically know the most about the market are powerless to act on their knowledge until they receive permission from the core.

The marketplace, on the other hand, is alive with dynamic transactions, complex relationships, and evolving ecosystems. It includes customers, shareholders, lenders, competitors, future employees, entrepreneurs, partners, and other players—all outside of your organization, and all beyond your control.

These forces, slow and bureaucratic vs. dynamic and cocreating, are like oil and water—they simply don't naturally mix. The slow response time between information transmission up the chain of command and decisions back down are major contributors to the rise in corporate failures since the 1970s. The structures that support the round-trip communication path from the perimeter to the top and back are simply unable to deal with the rate of change and complexity of today's digital ecosystems. The oil and water have to be disrupted, somehow shaken, to become integrated.

Unsurprisingly, the inability to move quickly on perimeter-provided information demoralizes those at the edge. Perimeter players are the ones who, day in and day out, are learning the most about the way the market is changing and what customers want. But they're organizationally stifled; they're unable to help the company create the value that would be generated if their information were acted on immediately. Instead, after they send the information to the top for processing, they wait helplessly for others to act on it, hoping the action will be fast enough to meet the new customer demand or market opportunity. All of which, of course, is why companies that persist in managing through such bureaucratic hierarchies are at great risk.

At this point you might be saying, "Hold on a minute. We're trying new approaches that get around the problem of slow core decision-making. We're using lean start-up and agile." And we agree that these frameworks and methods are a good way to begin the management transformation, because both use an iterative cycle of conceiving, building, and testing new products and services to promote continuous learning and empowered, cross-disciplinary decision-making. They do make experimentation part of the development process and they do reduce risk. But to what degree?

Normally when lean and agile are implemented in large enterprises, centralized planning and decision-making remain at the heart of the way the company conducts business. Companies tend to implement them in the *context of existing systems and processes*. Teams may be empowered to make certain predefined decisions, but the authority, power, and strategic decisions remain locked in bureaucracy. Still, a world without traditional management does not mean a world without managers, as many agile advocates propose. (We address in Chapter 8 just how valuable, if underused, your middle managers are today.)

What companies need now is a management system that can get them to Wave 3, one that lets peripheral teams act on what they know rather than sending it up the pyramid for processing. Without compromising corporate goals and business outcomes, peripheral teams need the autonomy to operationalize strategy through experimentation and rapid response to market feedback — in other words, *agility*. But how?

Company leaders need a way to first, break the cycle of centralized decision-making, and second, hold teams accountable for achieving outcomes that deliver the company's strategies and goals. To illustrate, we begin by examining the digital natives, companies that started their organizational life in the digital world.

The solution to the crisis of management is the outcome of the rise of cloud-native companies, full of engineers with an open-source mindset and growing like crazy. As they built their companies, they reinvented the tools of management, hiring and promotion practices, and organizational design. How did they do this, and what does that mean to management today?

As products and services were built to use the emerging Web economy, and digital tools modernized product development, a revolutionary way of managing work emerged. Internet-based companies, the cloud natives, tailored their management practices to the realities of automated coordination, continuous change, and complex market ecosystems. Engaged workers, linked to the market and acting on feedback, enabled three new control mechanisms for corporate management: self-management, self-governance, and self-organization. It is these that are the *how* of management and organizational transformation from Wave 0 to Wave 3!

SELF-MANAGEMENT: AUTONOMY WITH ACCOUNTABILITY

Management knowledge and skills must be learned and employed by everyone in the company in order to execute the transformation to Wave 2. To achieve Wave 2 team autonomy, self-management pushes the traditional functions of management—planning, coordinating, controlling, and staffing—directly into the teams, be they technology teams, business teams, or product development teams. Old control mechanisms must also be updated, which means jettisoning out-of-date roles, techniques, methods, and practices. Establishing clear roles, being accountable, building trust, making trade-offs, collaborating, cooperating, making collective decisions, allocating resources, prioritizing learning, and delivering results—all of these skills are necessary for autonomous teams; unfortunately, we do not see them being practiced in most large enterprises—yet.

Notice that we haven't gotten rid of hierarchy in Wave 2, only bureaucracy. Hierarchy, in fact, works well when we include horizontal collaboration and not just vertical alignment. Horizontal links are enabled by *boundary spanners,* people who work across organizational and functional borders. Characteristics of boundary spanners include: the ability to influence others, to encourage diverse thinking, and to emphasize inclusion, collaboration, communication, and cooperation. Spanning boundaries reinforces exploration and experimentation, resulting in innovative products and services as well as evolutionary organizational structures, practices, and processes.

Boundary spanning also supports accountability. In large corporations, people often specialize in their business, product, or function; unaware of opportunities or dependencies in adjacent spaces. This reduces accountability for removing dependencies, finding synergies, and transferring knowledge across internal organizational boundaries. Hence the rigidity of organizational silos. But when dependencies across teams, functions, or products are based on relationships between people, work, once defined by managers, is negotiated between colleagues. Boundary spanners increase accountability by brokering communication between groups, sharing knowledge and feedback, and introducing new ideas to others.

Of course when we challenge executives to introduce self-management, democratize decision-making, and amplify autonomy, we encounter resistance. They rarely think their company or its employees are ready for self-management. They don't trust the human system to be responsible and accountable, and they may not want to give up their control. Since this is the first major step for large, traditional organizations that want to embark on the digital wave journey, it helps to explore the immediate benefits of self-management.

Human beings have a deep biological need to accurately predict and control their world, so they are happier when they have a sense of power over their work. In other words, autonomy. When *teams* can openly and honestly negotiate their commitments, they are much more likely to deliver. This doesn't mean that we are moving toward anarchy. In fact, autonomy, a sense of choice and *personal* control, produces less stress and improves coping skills while inspiring people to achieve their goals and sustain new behaviors. Conversely, lack of autonomy produces disengagement, negativity, and apathy.[6] Which of these truly leads to anarchy?

Further, autonomy enables teams to use simple rules, heuristics, and experiments to form and test hypotheses that validate their assumptions and expectations. They run these experiments and analyze the results—then learn and apply what they've learned to design succeeding experiments. This allows teams to incorporate learning into novel technical and organizational solutions that fuel the digital transformation and break down bureaucracy.

But autonomy requires that authority, decision-making, and often even funding be distributed rather than centralized. When we leave behind centralized planning and bureaucracy, however, we need to provide people time to think—to have a point of view and communicate their perspectives. Thinking is work, work that can turn into conversations that spark innovation, which generates value; and value creation requires ownership.

Greater ownership of outcomes, implicit in self-management, produces conversations that enable collaboration and generate fresh ideas, the breeding ground of innovation. Self-managing teams find time to tap into conversations, e-mails, meetings, lunches, or even chance commuting encounters to remove confusion and harness innovation and change. They constantly ask: "What do we need to do collectively today?" And while bureaucracies produce cascading error, self-management produces better decisions. In other words, errors at higher levels are amplified as they move down the chain of command in bureaucracies, while self-management avoids amplifying errors by pushing decision-making down and utilizing horizontal social connections to overcome technical and organizational dependencies. From Wave 2 on,

---

6 Heidi Grant Halvorson, *No One Understands You and What to Do About It* (Boston: Harvard Business Review Press, 2015), Kindle ed., location 2003.

decisions that require local expertise, especially those involving tasks that are highly interdependent and time critical, are better made by the people who are working at the point of solution.

Finally, self-managed teams are able to operate like high-reliability organizations, such as nuclear power plants, emergency rooms, hostage negotiation teams, surgery teams, and aircraft carrier landing crews.[7] As autonomy increases, these teams learn to recognize weak signals, small clues that something is wrong or that the unexpected is about to happen. Reliability requires team members to report, discuss, and remove these errors and mistakes when noticed. In the safe environment that self-management produces, people learn how to report and make good decisions based on small mistakes and feedback.

With Wave 2 technology well established, automation, cloud, and containers have turned behemoths of code into manageable units. This allows business to speed up to the pace of continuous deployment. Replacing bureaucracy with a healthy hierarchy has enabled the new roles and lean-agile practices to become more widespread. The organization has loosened up enough to realize the fruits of experimentation: innovation and boundary-spanning collaboration. Now corporate leaders must take on the challenges of governance.

SELF-GOVERNANCE:
PRODUCT DEVELOPMENT COMMUNITIES AND NETWORKS

As corporations push management skills and responsibility to agile teams, middle managers are freed up to take on challenges that create previously unavailable value. This coincides with the technical ability of a business to personalize customer interactions, releasing a

---

7   Karl E. Weick and Kathleen M. Sutcliffe, *Managing the Unexpected: Resilient Performance in an Age of Uncertainty*, 2nd ed. (San Francisco: Jossey-Bass, 2007).

plethora of tailored offers, products, and services. Today we experience this as being able to design a custom car, but tomorrow most of this customization will be invisible—under the hood—occurring as we shop and interact with our favorite websites, brands, and companies. Collectively these technical advances set the stage for a new corporate structure to emerge: horizontal, boundary-spanning networks.

While increased experimentation in a bureaucracy means an increased risk of errors that accumulate and cascade down the layers, in networks errors are reduced or even prevented through connectivity and fast information flow. Networks also have the capacity to isolate and contain unexpected events and, when less urgent, mobilize problem-solving communities.

This ability to form and dissipate is a huge advantage that networks have over more permanent hierarchical structures. Still, this knowledge was not really useful until recently, for though network organizations had been suggested in the past, this was before we had the technology to make them desirable and viable. Now, we have the resources (middle managers) and business structure (end-to-end product development units) to make them not only useful, but preferable. *And*, we surely have the need: digital.

Wave 3 companies have three key needs that require networks to harvest the value of their newfound agility: First, they need to find where information and skills lie within their gigantic pool of knowledge resources. Second, information has to flow without friction between all these people so they can quickly and easily contribute to work, even outside their immediate location. Third, they need to restructure the middle layers of hierarchy that have limited use and which are *no longer* the primary means of communication, decision-making, and information flow.

Establishing intentional networks, as opposed to relying on informal social networks, allows companies moving from Wave 1 to

Wave 3 technology to meet these needs. By linking middle managers across a large corporation, knowledge and information begin to flow in all directions. Loosely coupled teams can ask for and receive information and support from anywhere, not just their localized part of the company. Additionally, as customers provide feedback on products and services, real-time data begins to flow. Organizational networks can enable business to constantly adjust while avoiding bottlenecks and overwhelmed teams.

But how do we control all this autonomous activity — teams self-managing, middle managers functioning as network nodes, and digital teams fabricating new microservices that businesses combine in novel ways to experiment in the market with real customers? *Self-governance* provides the mindset, the skills, and the structure needed. Welcome to the collective commons.

Even within Wave 3 corporations, knowledge and resources are finite and can be overutilized. New research on the dynamics of the collective commons provides insight on how to manage limited resources using self-governance. To explore this, we look at research that won Elinor Ostrom the Nobel Prize in Economics. Seeking the underlying principles that make the collective commons an effective governing model, Ostrom found that they were: diversity and inclusion, effectively wielded informal power, the authority to police themselves, and the ability to quickly respond to external events impacting the community. Moreover, members of the commons most often put the community's interests before their own self-interest. This encourages the emergence of a community-based network infrastructure and the connectivity and reciprocity to support these collective behaviors (see sidebar).[8]

---

8 Jeremy Rifkin, *The Zero Marginal Cost Society: The Internet of Things, the Collaborative Commons, and the Eclipse of Capitalism* (Boston: St. Martin's Griffin, 2015).

Ostrom identified **seven design principles** for governing healthy and resilient collective commons and for managing shared resources:

~ Clearly define the boundaries of who is a member of the commons and who is not.

~ Establish rules, such as a charter, for using shared resources to avoid overuse or scarcity (think burnout and slow response times).

~ Collectively establish and adapt the rules that govern members and the commons as conditions change.

~ Monitor the activities and behaviors on the commons, through members of the commons and not outsiders.

~ Address violation of the rules of the commons but avoid overly punitive sanctions that generate ill will and poor participation.

~ Include access to third-party facilitation in the charter for conflict resolution when needed.

~ Ensure that governance by commons members is recognized by other forms of governance (such as corporate), or the ability to self-manage and self-govern is at risk.

True to the idea of collective agreements, the more individuals who actively participate in the commons, the higher its value to each participant.[9] Participation in the commons begins with agreed-upon self-management and governance protocols that generate collaboration, trust, and feedback. This enables social norming, peer coaching, and positive social physics. According to Jeremy Rifkin, "If there is an

---

9 For leaders, the value of the commons is supported by the literature on participative leadership.

essential theme to the commons, it is that the people who know best
how to govern their lives are the members of the community."[10] This
is true of alpine villages, DevOps teams, platform ecosystems, Etsy,
eBay, Facebook, Google . . . *and* traditional corporations.

Many software developers will recognize these attributes, along
with Ostrom's seven design principles, as similar to the environment of open-source communities.[11] As more large enterprises
transform across the waves, the knowledge and experience gained
by open-source communities, such as Apache Software Foundation
and the Linux Foundation, can be further put to use in developing
corporate self-governance.

When adopting self-governance, the size of the group governing itself is as important as the commons charter. According to the
British anthropologist Robin Dunbar, social relationships begin to
lose their cohesiveness when a group's participants exceed a certain
numerical threshold, typically between 100 and 250 individuals. Bill
Gore, the founder of high-tech product company W. L. Gore and
Associates, uses this concept to structure his company. Gore's build-
ings are built to hold 150 employees, and when a building becomes
full, they build a new one.[12]

When companies are very large and evolving into distributed
networks, Dunbar sees new challenges. As he puts it, relationships
"across very big units then become very casual — and don't have

---

10   Rifkin, op. cit., 161.

11   For more information, see the Linux governance commons at
     https://wiki.p2pfoundation.net/Linux_-_Governance and
     http://www.ics.uci.edu/~wscacchi/Papers/New/Jensen-Scacchi-OSS10.pdf.

12   NPR, "Don't Believe Facebook; You Only Have 150 Friends," *All Things
     Considered*, June 5, 2011, http://www.npr.org/2011/06/04/136723316/dont-believe-
     facebook-you-only-have-150-friends.

that deep meaning and sense of obligation and reciprocity that you have with your close friends."[13] One way to solve for this is to encourage the formation of self-governing Communities of Practice (CoPs), a concept social scientists Etienne Wenger and Jean Lave developed.[14]

CoPs are loosely connected, self-managing, and self-governing content-based networks that advance their practice in the context of daily work. While based on social relationships, their focus is on the *practice* of the members—shared frameworks, collective resources, and common perspectives. This emphasizes learning by doing, based on interdependencies of knowledge rather than interdependencies of tasks. What energizes a CoP is the discovery that its members face similar problems and bring diverse data, tools, and approaches for solving them to the community. This combination of social interactions and cross-domain conversations provides members new ways of making sense of change and new information, which drives innovation.

Communities of Practice enable a distributed, laterally scaled, peer-to-peer work environment—perfect for product development teams operating with Wave 2 and 3 technologies. They produce a company composed of thriving interdisciplinary teams that are cross-functional, cross-organizational, and technically diverse. The principles of the collective commons enable different parts of the company to manage and make trade-offs involving a set of common resources—people, time, budget, knowledge, outcomes, and

---

13 NPR, "Don't Believe Facebook; You Only Have 150 Friends." https://www.npr. org/2011/06/04/136723316/dont-believe-facebook-you-only-have-150-friends

14 Etienne Wenger, *Communities of Practice: Learning, Meaning, and Identity*, Learning in Doing: Social, Cognitive, and Computational Perspectives (Cambridge, MA: Cambridge University Press, 1999).

so on. Self-governance prioritizes collective use of these resources over individual needs. This eliminates walls and turf, "not my problem" thinking, competition for resources, and the authoritarian act of forcing others to accept one "right" way of doing things.

As members participate in their community, they come to value one another and the diversity and inclusivity of the commons. This generates social capital, the bond of self-governing teams, and asks: "If I do this, whom will it affect? With whom do I need to coordinate in order to avoid unintended consequences for myself and others?" It openly acknowledges, "We're all in this together. I need to support others so that they can support me."

Through frequent, focused interactions, the community begins to make decisions interdependently and use resources to the benefit of the whole.[15] Social cohesion—expanded trust and trustworthiness—develops because of open information sharing and strong personal relationships. The positive benefits of networks are amplified, including reciprocity, knowledge creation, and, ultimately, innovation. Collaboration becomes the means for producing value and creating and nourishing ecosystems. And these are not just ecosystems of developers; they are end-to-end business units (sales, marketing, customer services, field operations) that extend to external partners, suppliers, and customers—all cocreating value, products, and services.

If autonomous groups of 150 people, typical of an end-to-end product development unit, are to collaborate to generate value, they must self-manage and self-govern. All that remains then is to figure out who belongs in the 150. This brings us to the concept of self-organization.

---

15 Arbinger Institute, *The Outward Mindset: Seeing Beyond Ourselves* (San Francisco: Berrett-Koehler, 2016).

SELF-ORGANIZATION:
STABILITY WITH LOCAL ADAPTABILITY

In Wave 3 and beyond, we need networks that not only govern themselves but that also self-organize. Self-organization generates a corporate system that *thrives* in volatility, uncertainty, complexity, and ambiguity (VUCA). In place of silos, boundaries and interfaces are open, semipermeable—like those of living cells. The organization actively takes in new information, which it needs to maintain its state at the edge of chaos, and flows that information through teams, networks, and businesses. Structures are loosely coupled and easily reconfigured to adapt in an unscripted fashion to unpredictable internal and external opportunities, just like the Wave 3 technology.

In their seminal work on the dynamics of innovation, Ikujiro Nonaka and Hirotaka Takeuchi characterized self-organizing teams as: up to 30 members, from diverse functional backgrounds, acting autonomously, intentionally spanning internal and external corporate boundaries (boundary spanners), and working to achieve a shared goal.[16] The ability of people and teams to self-organize creates huge potential for large enterprises, particularly when they are functioning in and beyond Wave 3. These benefits come from the composable universe of products and services they contain, the high degree of diversity of people and knowledge, and the similarity of performance metrics and success criteria (strategies and goals). All that is needed to reap the rewards of self-organization are fast feedback loops (networks), leaderless control (self-management and self-governance), and the ability to operate far from equilibrium (agility).

---

16 *The Knowledge-Creating Company: How Japanese Companies Create the Dynamics of Innovation* (New York: Oxford University Press, 1995).

The most obvious benefit of self-organizing systems is their ability to absorb and survive disruption, even extreme disruption. When turbulence is introduced into self-organizing systems, the system behaves in unique, often surprising ways. Organizationally, when disruption hits and VUCA is created, it is absorbed as the system adapts, self-organizing agility. This produces an interesting, if often uncomfortable, paradox for leaders and managers: Stability is the primary quality of the system as a whole, yet the parts (businesses and products) undergo continuous, dynamic change. Enterprise agility means that stability at the corporate level is combined with instability and adaptability at the local level. By allowing self-organization, change—even transformation—becomes the hallmark of your company.

As a result, the ability to self-organize maintains the organization at the edge of chaos: able to move toward more order, focusing internally on a few key goals; or toward less order, focusing externally and incorporating customer feedback. Self-organizing networks take advantage of multiple domains of information and knowledge to quickly and fluidly analyze a situation and act. They coordinate cross-boundary activities without friction and are resilient, adapting to challenge and opportunity.

Although this form of structuring work and teams is just emerging, self-organizing networks enable Wave 3 technology. In the digital environment, near real-time information and feedback flow from markets, competitors, customers, and company strategy to inform product development networks. Self-organization enables these networks to respond by rapidly incorporating this feedback into products, services, and experiences they can test in the market. Working this way accelerates value creation, reduces bottlenecks, and increases collaboration.

So while digital transformation requires organizational networks and structures to continuously evolve in response to technical and market advances, self-organization provides the means to achieve this. Beyond Wave 3 we imagine corporate agility is structured as networks of networks. But, like digital transformation, this is a journey, and as large enterprises become hypertext organizations, we will learn to ask the right questions, frame good hypotheses, and validate our assumptions. Today we know that we need to radically transform the broader organizational context and processes. But how to remove the hierarchy that the hypertext organization allows and shift the mindset of thousands of people around the globe (including external partners, shareholders, and Wall Street), remains to be seen.

Whatever the organizational structure of Wave 4 and beyond, the hypertext company's ability to eliminate the old paradigm of the corporation as machine is key. Digital is pushing business far from the static, top-down management practices we have today toward those that operate within dynamic, constantly adapting, living ecosystems. This is the alternative to central control, and the next generation of management.

What we need now are the means for integrating the technical and organizational transformations that the digital journey requires. Fortunately, we don't have to invent a completely new management system from scratch. Several visionary leaders over the last 15 years have pioneered proven management frameworks that enable large companies to install autonomous teams while ensuring strategic alignment, accountability, and breakthrough performance. This is what we cover in Section II, right after we meet someone who has made the digital transformation journey.

Chapter 4

Navigating the Digital Tsunami

A few years ago the VP of an operations group inside a major telecommunications company reached out to us to help him deliver a change that focused on three things: the shift to agile delivery teams, the organization's culture, and his leadership team. The leadership team of five directors and eight managers managed 120 employees who performed customer-critical operations work (for example, 911 and corporate joint venture operations!). They also had multiple business partners (internal and external).

Along with some of his managers, the VP—we'll call him Joe—had participated in an Adaptive Leadership workshop delivered to the entire product engineering division (more than 150 managers). With the intent of reducing micromanagement, decreasing excessive interruption (shoulder taps), and establishing a culture of trust and collaboration, he had a vision of radically improving performance and results by changing the existing subject matter expert (SME) command-and-control management style to one of "manager as coach."

Joe was ready to rethink everything: roles, responsibilities, workflow, team structures, resource allocation, culture, business relationships, cross-organizational cooperation . . . everything. Getting started, Joe was already aware of a crucial characteristic of the digital revolution: There are no well-trodden paths and roads. The digital natives, who seem to be on a superhighway, started as trailblazers. And they are still trailblazing. They beckon the rest of us to get going, to join the journey and participate in the digital world. All well and good. But where to start, and what should you look for to indicate you are on the right path?

For Joe, realizing that he wanted to chart a course with his management team that they could navigate together meant that the journey would unfold due to their actions and learning. With that said, let's look at the steps that guide the archetypal Surge journey, steps that, as we will see, also guided the journey Joe and his entire group effectively took as they moved from Wave 0 to Wave 1 and dramatically changed their culture—all through two corporate reorgs and a failed merger—in just eight months.

NAVIGATIONAL PLOT POINT #1: CREATE A VISION FOR THE COLLECTIVE

The first step in the archetypal Surge journey belongs to senior executives. Working with seasoned internal and/or external transformation practitioners, these leaders need to consider and develop directional artifacts that they can share with their organization. We find four steps help leaders navigate this stage of their journey:

First, analyze how your current system is functioning; identify bottlenecks, accidental adversaries, and positive/negative feedback loops. This builds a view of the organizational systems that are producing the norms, relationships, and culture. We typically use causal loop diagrams to capture the dynamics of the organizational system

(Figure 4.1). This allows managers to see root causes and visually understand how they are part of the problem as well as the solution. These maps also provide the means for identifying levers of change, i.e., places in the system where small changes can produce big results.

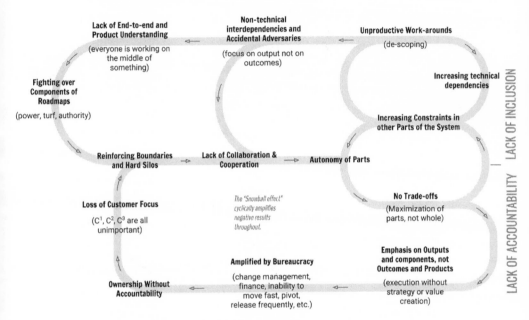

Figure 4.1. **A system map typical of large corporations in Waves 0 and 1.**

Next, imagine your future, an aspirational end state that makes the transformation real and meaningful to everyone. For digital transformation this must be more than a technical journey. The organizational transformation required to support and enable the technology is what captures the hearts and minds of your colleagues (recall Figures 2.1 and 2.3). Your vision of the new organization, and how it will impact the engagement and contribution of all employees, creates the adaptive transformational journey that you are taking.

Write a vision statement, a narrative that invites everyone to participate, makes the case for the journey, and forecasts not only the inevitable hardships you might encounter, but how you will overcome them. Unleash your passion here, for this is your manifesto. Even if the rest of the company doesn't change, what actions can you take, and how do they make work more exciting for the whole organization and beneficial to your customers? Your future end state should enable end-to-end product development, redesign outdated processes, and overcome organizational fragmentation and rigid boundaries.

One leadership team imagined a future for their customers and employees and used it to restructure their organization and products (Table IV.I). This became the foundation for their adoption of lean-agile practices, and they built both technical and adaptive transformation backlogs to achieve these outcomes. In the process they redesigned how teams interacted across a geographically dispersed product development unit and moved from funding projects to funding products — a significant benefit to their business partners.

Table IV.I: **A future end state imagined by leaders in a financial corporation.**

CUSTOMER EXPERIENCE	EMPLOYEE EXPERIENCE
Wow, this was a helpful interaction.	Test and learn experiments are well designed and executed.
I didn't realize I could do this so easily.	We all understand our strategy and spend time delivering it.
Each interaction experience feels relevant to the moment I contact them.	Investments are evidence-based and customer-centered.
Quality of content is exceptionally high, these folks get me.	We have the ability to stop work that does not generate customer value.

Now, create a *new* system map (Figure 4.2), one that shows how this future world will function. Make sure any structural changes you make produce the operating model you need to achieve your vision. Look for potential bottlenecks, points where decision making might slow, and any places where human interactions could generate accidental adversaries. Often this map highlights the need to transform centralized corporate functions like finance, planning, or change management. Working with them to change *their* processes is a key role of leaders during transformation.

Finally, ask yourself: How have I (or we) participated in the creation of the organization, culture, and performance we have today? The systems perspective reveals that today's problems come from yesterday's solutions because cause and effect are not clearly or closely related in time and space.[1] Most executives have been in leadership positions for years and they are living with the decisions they made and actions they took years ago. When leaders realize that the organizational system is operating perfectly from a systems perspective, they begin to see their impact on the system. To lead transformation they must see that the relationships and culture they seek to change are produced by the existing organizational structure and how it is functioning. Systemic change requires, first, that leaders change their behaviors and commitments before the rest of the organization can transform.

Critical to navigating this part of the transformational journey is to understand the status quo and what holds the system there. This reveals both stabilizing and destabilizing forces that must be dampened and amplified respectively. Often, at the beginning of the journey, stabilizing forces overpower the destabilizing

---

1   Peter F. Senge, *The Fifth Discipline: The Art & Practice of the Learning Organization*, rev. ed. (New York: Doubleday, 2006).

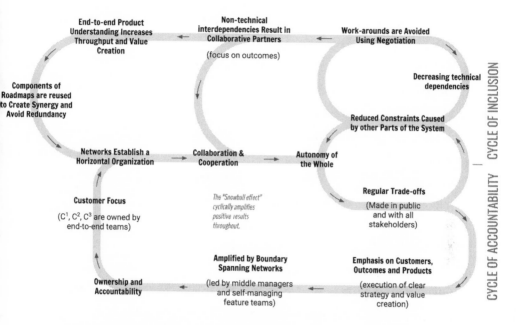

Figure 4.2. **One example of transforming the system in Figure 4.1.** (Though often the new system appears very different from the existing one, this example uses the same flows for ease of understanding.).

ones, maintaining the status quo and causing the change initiative to fail. This balance must be reversed for the transformational journey to be sustainable. Just as being able to recognize the signs of stabilization keeps you from ending up back at the status quo, knowing the forces of destabilization allows you to intentionally amplify disruption.

With all this reflection and reimagining you can write a story of your desired future that is visceral, compelling, and exciting (Chapter 5) . . . rather than a wish list. Your goal is to enroll others, to give people room to contribute to the narrative. Tell everyone about it — communicate until you are hoarse. Let people revise it on the spot, with your coaching, so that they can tell their version of the journey to others and begin a groundswell. Work with any and all individuals, teams, and groups within your organization. Have an open door policy when it comes to talking about the journey you are taking.

NAVIGATIONAL PLOT POINT #2:
FORGE THE COMMITMENT OF SENIOR LEADERS

A gentle reminder to executives: You can't do this alone. It takes everyone to adopt a digital strategy and to make it sustainable. The first people you need to enlist are members of your senior leadership team (SLT). Regardless of the size of your transformational effort, your senior leaders need to become a high-performing team committed to your vision and the need to transform. In addition to the strategic aspects of transformation, much of the heavy lifting falls on their shoulders. Many of them will need to mature their leadership styles and adopt new roles, delegating many of their activities to others so they can perform more strategic work.

The Surge journey for the SLT naturally flows through three stages: relating, thinking, and doing. Relating, the first stage, addresses the personal obstacles and role-related challenges that exist between individuals on the team. Use facilitated team workshops to generate in-depth knowledge of self, teammates, and transformational roles and responsibilities. Relating requires more than superficial updates on what each person intends to do to transform. These are conversations that address how "our" actions and behaviors have produced the systemic challenges you've mapped and why they must change; consequently, these are often the hardest conversations managers and executives will ever have.

During the relating stage, the SLT has the opportunity to address misperceptions they have about each other, resolve any historical adversarial relationships, and develop their emotional intelligence, leadership maturity, and thinking styles. These conversations take time because they require being together to explore and resolve hidden agendas, resentments, fears, competition, power differentials, expectations, and personality differences. The safest and most productive way to move through this stage is to bring on an experienced executive coach or organizational psychologist to facilitate the workshops. The outcome and sign of a successful relating stage is an executive team committed to each other and to the journey that they are taking together.

As they forge their relationship with each other, team members move from thinking about themselves (working *in* transformation) to focusing on the organization (working *on* transformation). To ensure that the new organization will function in a way that achieves their vision, the SLT redirects their concentration toward designing a new organizational structure, something that only their team can do. Part of their challenge is to preserve key relationships and knowledge networks. Often people can be "re-roled" — which is less traumatic and enables personnel changes without loss or a reorg. This new organization will change your relationships with the rest of the company, your closest stakeholders, and business partners, and these changing interactions need to be addressed proactively by bringing these partners into the process.

Digital transformation is often tech initiated, requiring leaders to enlist their business partners and causing them to begin their own transformational journey. But regardless of where digital transformation is initiated, the level of technical *and* business readiness determines the journey you are taking and the work you must do together. The goal is to transform together, not to race ahead of one another. Decisions about the degree of technical change (Are we headed to Wave 3?), adoption of one or multiple agile methodologies, and the tools to be used for documenting, tracking, and communicating must be jointly made. Now is also the time to ensure that you have a deep understanding of the customer experience/journey so that technologists can design the outcomes they desire.

The thinking stage can also reveal previously unseen areas of necessary transformation. Key influencers and subject matter experts are identified and recruited to the working sessions to address these challenges as they arise. This ensures that everyone stays together, not chasing 10 different versions of the future.

As the vision becomes more concrete, the SLT moves into the final stage: doing. They are now able to describe what success looks like from the perspective of team members, the rest of the organization, business partners, the company, and customers. The doing stage articulates a strategy and develops milestones for navigating to the first digital wave on your journey, producing the first transformative workflows and action plans. Change agents are recruited and coached to spread the word and turn the plan into action.

This full process—relating, thinking, doing—repeated across the management hierarchy, removes bureaucracy and produces dramatic change without reorg, HR involvement, or major disruption of existing social networks. It is the first iteration of a new organizational structure, the journey from bureaucracy to ecosystem. Most importantly, it is built from careful consideration of *organizational* changes that are needed and the benefits they create relative to the market and customer ecosystems. This sets the stage for technical changes to be initiated at the team level.

Forging the Commitment of Senior Leaders has four outcomes: First, it creates a strategy to amplify destabilizing forces and dampen stabilizing forces so that the transformation begins without a lot of resistance—and it "publishes" this plan: The end state vision is made public, often using town halls and graphics, which lets people clearly see that they can't get to the future with just the behaviors, processes, and skills they're currently enlisting.

Secondly, leaders now have a list of what to jettison, what to conserve, and what to improve or modify. It is easy to identify existing processes and workflow that need to change, but harder to pinpoint work habits and assumptions, leadership behaviors, and cultural norms that are holding you back. The changes on your list also impact core corporate functions like change management, finance and resource allocation, and product governance. Be ready to work across organizational boundaries to address things that impact others.

Third, you learn who you can rely on to drive change. You have identified the positive deviants and change agents in your organization and across the company. This creates a diverse leadership network that can guide the organization as teams integrate the transformation into the existing work they must deliver.

Fourth, you've produced a set of high-level milestones that turn the vision into a mission on which everyone can act.

The outcomes of engaging senior leadership are both personal and action oriented. They are as much about self-awareness and growth as they are about developing a narrative or a picture that describes the intent of the transformation and a high-level plan for achieving it. Establishing a SLT unified in heart and mind and committed to each other and the journey it leads is critical; this is what the relating, thinking, doing stages accomplish. Having been through these experiences, the SLT can lead similar conversations with other leaders, middle managers, and teams, coaching them to change, spread the word, enroll others, and amplify the transformation.

One team we worked with created a series of "flyover maps" of the terrain (Figure 4.3) as it morphed from a current state to their desired future. This provided a compelling step-by-step vision of the future, a visual narrative of the required interim states and final outcome (Figure 4.4). Visuals like these are powerful drivers of engagement and the emergence of a transformation built on creativity and imagination.

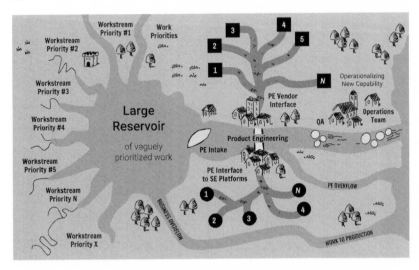

Figure 4.3. A terrain map that represents the obstacles of a value *stream* that begins with the business (work streams), moves past product engineering (PE) and systems/operations engineering (SE), and spills into production (ocean).

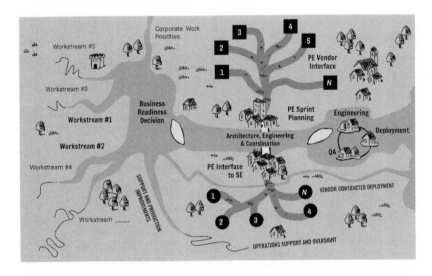

Figure 4.4. After five interim maps, the final terrain map depicts the future vision and the outcome of transformation of business and technology organizations.

NAVIGATIONAL PLOT POINT #3:
ENGAGE MIDDLE MANAGERS TO CHART THE COURSE

Middle managers are key to operationalizing the transformational strategy developed by the senior leadership team. Because middle managers moderate the experience of change for the rest of the company, they have the biggest impact on changing the culture and embedding agility into the organization. Of course their work is most powerful when it is a collective effort, when they can coach each other and learn from each other. Middle manager networks (Chapter 8) also have a broad understanding of how the organization creates value for customers and the company. They can calibrate the vision to meet their local needs and environments, introduce technical and adaptive experiments, and spread learning.

Deploying middle managers as connectors and boundary spanners improves horizontal collaboration, which spreads innovative ideas, removes duplication of effort, and solves problems quickly. Wherever needed, middle managers can also coach teams that are creating technical and innovative value by providing on-demand subject matter expertise (SME). This new use of managers as coaches improves team hygiene and provides the skills the teams need to become self-managing, self-governing, and, eventually, self-organizing. Engaging them kicks off the transformation and initiates change that fuels the evolution of the whole system.

JOE'S TRANSFORMATIONAL JOURNEY

Following the Adaptive Management workshop, Joe worked with us to understand his starting conditions. We mapped both his existing and desired systems, then we designed a new flow for how his organization might function. From this we prototyped the roles and responsibilities needed in the new organization and defined a structure that could deliver the workflow and operating model he sought. Now it was time to take the new system to his leadership team.

The challenge was to deliver the thinking we had done in a way that didn't reinforce the top-down, command-and-control management style that existed at the time. Our goal was for Joe's leadership team to find their own path to the outcomes we had imagined. This would expand our thinking, bringing in new ideas and experiences, and make the management team the owners of the transformation journey.

Joe's management team and employees had been trapped in an environment of high-pressure work that was in constant volatility, uncertainty, complexity, and ambiguity (VUCA): unrealistic delivery deadlines, constantly changing priorities, perceived lack of resources, and overwhelming amounts of customer-critical work. People were emotionally exhausted, burned out, and frustrated. We started by helping the management team realize that this reality was not normal, and that no one was going to swoop in and save them; that to change the situation they would need to take ownership and do the hard work of transformation.

The first four weeks of the engagement were unlike any that the organization or its managers had experienced. Teams were largely left to self-manage (which ignited the transformation for them) while their managers spent hours and days coming to grips with the situation and reinventing their organization. Without providing them Joe's artifacts, we moved them through the same thinking process that he had followed to reveal the problems of the status quo and enable them to envision a different, aspirational future.

Although it often seems obvious to others, most managers have little idea of the emotional conditions within their organizations and what they can and should do about unhealthy behaviors that can lead to high-stress cultures. For Joe's management team, resolving their own interpersonal issues and relationships had to precede anything they could do for their teams. The very candid and often emotional conversations that we facilitated gave the management team the ability to have authentic exchanges, first with each other and then with their colleagues. Inevitably, this reshaped how they saw themselves and how they worked with each other. In the meantime, teams were kept informed about the process, and their questions and concerns were integrated into the conversations managers had.

As the management team moved out of the relating stage and into thinking and doing, key influencers from the tech teams were invited into the conversation. This was particularly important during a two-day session to create new roles and responsibilities for directors, managers, team leads, and team members. Participants broke out into groups composed of people from all four roles in the organization, and together they examined each role and defined its responsibilities and activities. Each group presented its work to the whole and a final version was crafted. Joe stayed away, letting them define their new system on their own.

The results were impressive. Managers became *people leaders*, responsible for coaching and developing individuals and teams as well as *collectively* managing the hiring process, yearly reviews, and promotions (eliminating a significant source of accidental adversaries). Directors became *portfolio leaders*, strategic partners for the businesses. They were responsible for eliminating shoulder taps and for prioritizing commitments by negotiating trade-off between business partners. *Program lead* became a new rotational non-management role chosen by each team and responsible for leading the teams as they turned business commitments into a prioritized team backlog. They also negotiated with each other to share resources so that heroics and self-sacrifice became unnecessary and team members had the opportunity to learn and utilize new skills and knowledge.

It was now time to align team backlogs to business commitments. Portfolio leaders reconfirmed existing commitments with their business partners—in this case without changing deadlines or adding resources. This produced 10 commitments that the organization had to deliver by the end of the year, which was nearly half over—a daunting task, but one that the organization was up to . . . for they had a plan:

With program leads representing their teams, and people leaders observing but not participating, all team backlogs were placed in a "holding pen." Behind every program leader was a blank flip chart, which represented his or her new backlog.

Beginning with the first commitment, portfolio and program leads responsible for delivering the outcome described their work, challenges, obstacles, and needs. Portfolio leaders clarified the business requirements, and other program leads noted where their team's work or support was necessary to deliver the commitment. That work was placed on the appropriate backlog flip charts. Program leads collectively overcame impediments and resolved problems, partially by moving some of the work to a managed services partner.

This process was repeated until all 10 commitments were completed and each team had a prioritized backlog aligned to the organization's business commitments. At the end of the session, program leads reviewed the holding pen and determined what they wanted to add to their backlogs and in what priority. The group decided that what remained in the holding pen would be completed in a Kanban scheduling fashion when time permitted.

Observing the two-day workshop, Joe was, "Thrilled; and I've never used that word before." Everyone checked out with feelings of accomplishment and unity that were amplified when the work was presented at an all-hands meeting and was greeted with uniform agreement and applause.

Because no delivery dates had been changed or resources added, the three leadership groups decided to meet weekly to coordinate, communicate, and resolve any problems that threatened their commitments. These *triple P* meetings (i.e., portfolio, program, and people) contributed to delivery of all 10 commitments by year's end. During the process, the culture changed, and the next year, with 95 percent of employees responding to the internal employee survey, the transformation was visible — a shift from red and yellow the year before to overwhelmingly green. Embedding the ability to transform into this organization also enabled it to redesign itself again 18 months later, this time without the need for external coaching.

Joe's organization made a massive internal shift: Managers overcame their contentious relationships with each other; the management model became based on coaching teams rather than on SME status; and strategic relationships with corporate business partners deepened. Perhaps the most important part of the transformation was cultural, reflected in a work environment that became collegial and collaborative. Within that environment everyone focused on continuously improving the organization by working *on* as well as *in* it; they owned their experience of their organization. The transformation was dynamic, and management continued to redesign the operating model and structure of the organization.

This is the ultimate benefit of the *Surge* model: Transformation creates an organization able to sense and respond to changes in the environment, whether these are a move to a new digital wave, a market shift that must be addressed, or a business opportunity that requires self-organizing or restructuring.

Learning to navigate transformational journeys is the key to perpetual adaptation, which is why living systems can thrive in uncertainty and respond to changes in their environment. Machines can't do this. Every time you catch yourself asking for a more detailed road map, or getting lost in the weeds of a project plan, or explaining that you are seeking to become a well-oiled machine, you are squeezing the life out of your organization. When this happens, just stop. Embrace the mess, triage the situation if it is urgent, and then move forward with curiosity, fearlessness, and perseverance.

"Preventing people from designing their world . . . robs them of what is essentially human . . . Participating in systems under continuous reconstruction by its constituents [is] a way of realizing oneself in coordination with others."

—Klaus Krippendorff,
The Cybernetics of Design and the Design of Cybernetics

THE JOURNEY OF DIGITAL TRANSFORMATION

On June 1, 2011, a tornado ripped through the town of Monson, Massachusetts. It pulled trees out of the ground, flattened homes, and devastated the entire population of nearly 9,000. One resident hid in her downstairs closet, holding the door shut as the tornado roared above her. As she described it, "It felt like a freight train was coming through my backyard." As the storm moved into Brimfield State Forest, the tornado reached approximately one-half mile in width.[1]

Out of the wreckage rose two twentysomethings, Caitria and Morgan O'Neill, who pulled the community together. A year later,

---

[1] Tripline, "Path of the Springfield / Monson Tornado," accessed May 19, 2017, http://www.tripline.net/trip/Path_of_the_Springfield_/_Monson_Tornado-67260334774010039838AE02C8A41537.

the sisters discussed their experience from the TEDx Boston stage, explaining how they were able to save their town.

"We had to learn how to answer questions quickly and to solve problems in a minute or less; otherwise, something more urgent would come up, and it wouldn't get done," Caitria said.

"We didn't get our authority from the board of selectmen or the emergency management director or the United Way," Morgan added. "We just started answering questions and making decisions because someone — anyone — had to. And why not me?"[2]

These two statements capture the speed of operating in a Wave 3 digital environment.

After a major disaster, there are four to seven days in which disaster areas capture 50 percent of their aid. Because there are always new disaster sites that need attention, the money and supplies brought in early on must cover rebuilding for the next five years. Although large organizations like the Red Cross and United Way are essential, after they leave the locals are left to pick up the pieces, doing work that often totals millions of dollars and thousands of labor hours. The same thing happens when lean start-up trainers and agile coaches move on from a Wave 1 corporation, and the employees are left to figure out how to turn their experience into a corporate transformation.

Essentially, they need to do what Caitria and Morgan did: Organize a self-sustaining ecosystem that can be turned loose to run on its own . . . forever.

From day one the sisters worked themselves to exhaustion each day, showered in the shelter, and then got up to do it all over again.

---

2 TED, "How to Step up in the Face of Disaster" (TED Talk transcript), August 2012, https://www.ted.com/talks/caitria_and_morgan_o_neill_how_to_step_up_in_the_face_of_disaster/transcript?language=en#t-198180.

Throughout the recovery they were at the epicenter of a dynamic network of community members, keeping the whirl of activity moving and making split-second choices that enabled all the moving parts of Monson to act with autonomy. As they delegated, people delivered.

Recovering from disasters, community organizers lack the sophistication, experience, and resources of the Red Cross and United Way; a similar difference exists between you and your agile vendors. But what these communities have that you might not have is *purpose*. They are desperate to envision their community whole again, and their purpose generates real-time response and reveals unforeseen opportunities. When a bunch of terrified townspeople get together to solve their problems, they step outside their normal lives and operate in a world that follows a new set of rules. Each person in the ecosystem is a valued asset. Each helps to create the ecosystem's collective future reality. Purpose, autonomy, and action deliver the desired future.

The story of Monson illustrates a stable community ripped apart by nature, provided minimal resources, and then left to put the pieces back together to recreate a functioning community. The disaster is analogous to the current market, with technological and economic shifts threatening the future of traditional enterprises.

Pre-disaster Monson can be seen as the Wave 0 company, the tornado as the radically evolving markets and industries, and the first responders that the O'Neill sisters encountered as the initiators of and investments in digital transformation. The arrival and departure of the Red Cross and United Way mirror the aftermath of agile training or an executive visit to a digital native. Following the creative destruction, a few positive, deviant leaders (the O'Neill sisters) are all that remain to reassemble the human system into a functioning whole.

The problem, at least in part, has been exacerbated by the

assumption that all companies should be built the same, with the same kinds of structures and processes. What is good for Starbucks is also good for General Electric, or Verizon, or any other successful business. Most interventions tend to look at a company's public attributes (profit, margin, return on investment) rather than seeking to understand how the enterprise functions and then asking if it *should* be organized as it is.

The same happens during digital transformation. Your adoption of new computer languages and tools is not a measure of your ability to navigate the waves. While technically necessary, these do not enable the rest of the organization to transform. The initial structure that lean and agile creates will get you to Wave 1 and is a *prototype* for future waves. Then, as constraints and dynamic forces of the market and corporate context are applied, the structure is modified and adapts to the evolving required functionality. Once this is set in motion, form follows function, and the bureaucratic, mechanistic corporate structure evolves into a business heterarchy of self-organizing structures, each adapting to their unique market conditions.

When we view the organization as a living system capable of its own response to disruption, we begin to work with, not against, its dynamic nature. It is literally, not figuratively, an ecosystem. Its diverse, composable elements establish relationships that create value, knowledge, and innovation. Like the Monson community, the corporate ecosystem's interconnected parts are linked to an interdependent fate. What happens at one part of the ecosystem ripples through the whole, producing constant motion and adaptation. The company can and will respond in ways no one can predict—and the actions of every employee contribute to the outcome.

Soon, entire markets will be composed of Wave 3 companies. To join these market ecosystems, executives and employees have to see their company as a living, adaptive system. Everyone must embrace the new paradigm of the ecosystem, from the CEO all the way to the hourly worker. To survive, your organization must become fit for rapid, continuous change — and it must develop that fitness now. The assets your company needs to survive in the digital ecosystem are creativity and connection; it is in these that you generate speed and customer value. In *Surge* we provide critical foundational elements that corporations can use during digital transformation and while moving across the digital waves.

The concepts we present here are practical. They reduce bottlenecks. They allow leaders and teams to make sense of complexity without adding complicated processes. They produce collective actions and behaviors, shared commitments, and a web of healthy networks that allow you to deconstruct your bureaucratic and technical monoliths and turn them into vibrant, healthy business ecosystems.

Each chapter presents a primary component of digital transformation. They can be combined and recombined, accentuated during one phase of transformation and dampened during another. This creates the ability to start where you are and follow yes regardless of where you are in the corporation, designing a journey that fits the unique context of your environment.

Collectively, these chapters provide the *how* that large companies need to learn, to innovate, and to transform while continuing to operate with the complexity and scale of an established enterprise.

To help you to understand how to navigate the digital transformation, we introduce you to four representative leaders from four composite companies, each at a different point in the digital journey. We invite you to get to know them and follow the journey Abe takes both personally and organizationally as he leads his Wave 0 company as they initiate their digital transformation.

INTERMEZZO

A Conversation among Four Leaders — Abe's Dilemma and the Crucible of Leadership

Imagine a lunch conversation among four leaders who gather regularly to coach one another. Meet Abe, Anna, Gina, and Ethan. They have been talking about technology — the challenges and opportunities they're facing — when Abe brings the discussion around to something that has been taking over his world.

"We started transitioning to agile this month," says Abe. "It's a disaster."

Abe is a CIO in a large Fortune 50 financial services company that has been rooted firmly in Wave 0 for decades. Recently the company has begun tiptoeing toward Wave 1. This included the implementation of agile teams in parts of IT, which generated a steady stream of agile and lean experts who've been pounding Abe on the need to scale agile with more sophisticated process frameworks. He's also gotten a heavy dose of consulting advice on making sure everyone is "doing" agile correctly. His latest challenge is to accomplish a digital transformation that weaves together business and technology. This has him wondering how he will expand the transformation into the business side of the house. The only thing he is certain of as he begins this conversation is that this is going to be wildly disruptive to the existing organization — processes, projects, people, and structures.

Abe forces a pained chuckle and looks hopefully around the table at his colleagues. "You guys have all done this . . . help me out here."

Anna leads a large development group in a global entertainment company, now operating in Waves 3 and 4. Ethan leads IT for an established online consumer company, birthed in Wave 2 as a cloud-native company, now in Wave 3 and rapidly growing its market share. Gina works at a high-end clothing and accessories company, leading its e-commerce division. She led the transformation from a monolithic operating model to a product-centric platform that builds its offers using microservices. She began the agile journey in Wave 0 and is now fully operating in Wave 3.

"Well, you don't just 'become agile,'" Gina offers, emphasizing her words with air quotes. "You have to change your culture and organizational structure as well as people's hearts and minds. It's much more an adaptive challenge than it is a technical challenge. The big questions are: Are you willing to make the investment, of both time and money? And are your business partners on board and working with you?"

Hearing Gina's questions, Abe gives an almost imperceptible shrug.

"It didn't work for us at the start," she continues, remembering an adversarial relationship between business and technology. "Technically, the amount of technical debt we had made it tough. It was expensive to keep the monolithic infrastructure up and running, but thinking about blowing it up gave everyone cold feet."

Remembering this, Gina becomes quiet, staring out the window. She recalls asking her team to work more holistically when building software capabilities, forcing teams to consider the broader end-to-end user experience, and not simply chopping the work up into smaller units. She also recalls the heat she took for saying no when she was asked to extend major applications through a series of one-off projects that only made managing the already fragile systems even more complicated and difficult. The early effort was enormous, building all the necessary relationships (business, technology, finance, corporate strategy) to enable the organization to shift from a Wave 0 to a Wave 2 e-commerce company . . . but she had done it.

Ethan speaks up. "The real benefits of agile don't happen until you reduce bureaucracy. Nothing major will happen until the orga-nizational processes and controls loosen up. That's the only way IT can begin to operate as end-to-end feature teams. And it's the only way IT can become a partner to business in value creation, instead of just a cost center. The performance bump from team-level agility does little to drive a bigger impact to strategic objectives and the bottom line. Lucky for us, we didn't start with that problem."

Abe raises his eyebrows. "So why bother? When people ask me why we are doing this, what do I say? More importantly, what do I do? Some days I want to hide in my office and not come out."

"Honestly, agile teams and practices are the foundation to what you want to achieve," Ethan replies. "Your teams need to become respon-sible and accountable, not just for new software, but for real business outcomes. But here's the catch: This isn't the end game, it's merely the beginning of the journey. It's simply the first step toward transform-ing the mindsets, culture, and organizing principles throughout the company—how it organizes, collaborates, and innovates. Then the divide between business and technology can evaporate."

Ethan takes a moment to collect his thoughts before he contin-ues. "Working in a new way seems simple, but it's hard to implement when you're structured the way you are now. You work in a huge company, not a scrappy start-up. Every process and role needs to be reimagined to remove the bureaucracy and turf wars. Establishing agile teams is easy. Providing them with the backlogs to create prod-ucts that customers love, that's the challenge. When I left the corpo-rate world, we thought an app was a product! We had a lot to learn." Ethan smiles. "So . . . is it worth it? Are you kidding? If you were hon-est with yourself, you'd say your life sucks right now. You serve too many masters, and your teams are frustrated over how difficult it is to deliver real value. I get it. Staying where you are is unsustainable.

But imagine a future where all your teams work independently, enjoying the freedom to innovate, within *self*-imposed constraints. Nirvana, Abe. Really, that—not the stuff the consultants are peddling—is agility."

"But it is painful," Gina interjects, giving Abe an understanding look. "It might sound cliché, but the biggest challenge to transformation is you. I mean, are *you* ready for the personal transformation *you* need to lead your organization through Wave 1 and beyond? You have to help people unlearn the passive behaviors you've rewarded over the years. You have to help them learn to be decision makers, businesspeople, and part of a collaborative community."

Anna nods. "It's a serious question, Abe. You're going to need to leave behind a bunch of the leadership skills you've honed over your career. And if you think changing your leadership style is hard, believe me, getting your middle managers to change is even harder. You have to give them new jobs, new roles, new norms and rewards, as well as meaningful new ways to contribute . . . or nothing changes."

Abe nods and thinks for a moment. His mind feels like a pinball machine. He wants a single, clear answer, but he can't yet formulate a single, clear question. "How did you guys do it?" he asks at last.

"Here's the thing," Ethan says, noticing Abe's look. "*We* didn't do it. *Everyone* did it, together. There is no one way to do this. No silver bullet. No prescription. The first thing you do is be brutally honest; make sure you really understand where you are: You and your management team, working the way you work today, is what got you here. Success. But now it's probably holding you back. So you have to change, and you have to change the way others in the organization see you. *How* you change really depends on each interaction and conversation you have. Just remember, it's not about technology, it's about people."

"Transforming *can* be exhausting," Gina says. "You need to know how to lead *and* how to get out of the way — get out of the way of the people who will roll up their sleeves and make transformation happen. Digital waves constantly create new ways to do things. That's why you have to transfer a large degree of control to the people who are doing the work."

Abe nods pensively.

Gina continues, "That means equipping *everyone* in the company with the ability to lead, situation by situation. Empowerment, though, comes with greater accountability, probably a lot more than your managers and teams anticipate, certainly more than they're used to. Abe, you have to trust them . . . or you'll be in their way."

Abe wears a contemplative smile. Gina's words hit close to home.

"How are you going to lead this so the whole company transitions to greater agility?" Gina asks. "You're going to create the conditions that encourage people to reimagine your organization and then make their vision a reality."

Abe looks slightly pale. "It's definitely a new way of looking at things," he says. "Before, I could do this job almost without thinking. Now I'm thinking so much my head hurts."

"I have to go," Ethan says, calling for the check. "But I want to say one last thing: Moving through the waves highlights the human aspects of your company. You start this journey to solve production and speed issues, but you end up with teams of people who hold themselves accountable. We began hiring for mindset more than skill set. Our employees began to trust us, our business partners began to trust us, and we began to trust ourselves. Oh, and Abe, we're here for you. Text, phone . . . or buy lunch any day."

They all laugh, and Abe grabs the check.

Chapter 5

Social Memes —
Activate the Collective

In 2003 a single recording booth stood in Grand Central Terminal in New York City (Figure 5.1). It was illuminated with lights, its semitransparent walls glowing in patchy spots. Little red stick figures of people patterned the booth's surface. It had a metal door and a wheelchair ramp, a square window, and red letters stating "StoryCorps."

As commuters buzzed by, inside the structure sat two people with microphones and a list of questions; these were simply everyday people who had passed by and submitted to this . . . experiment. With the recorder rolling, the pair asked each other questions. For close to an hour they had an intimate conversation, the activity outside nearly, if not completely, forgotten. When the two were done, they received a copy of the audio, which was also delivered to the Library of Congress to be archived. This scenario was repeated over

Figure 5.1. **The StoryCorps booth in Grand Central Station, NYC.**

and over as busy people from all walks of life stopped long enough to have a conversation . . . to create their story.

"So we open this booth in one of the busiest places in the world and invite people to have this incredibly intimate conversation with another human being," StoryCorps founder Dave Isay said from the TED stage. "I had no idea if it would work, but from the very beginning it did. People treated the experience with incredible respect, and amazing conversations happened inside."[1]

Since that recording booth pilot project 15 years ago, StoryCorps has gathered the largest collection of human voices in history, growing steadily and with no sign of slowing down. As of this writing, it has released five books and won a $1 million MacArthur Award and a $1 million TED Prize, which the company used to launch an

---

1 TED, "Everyone around You Has a Story the World Needs to Hear" (TED Talk transcript), March 2015, https://www.ted.com/talks/dave_isay_everyone_around_you_has_a_story_the_world_needs_to_hear/transcript?language=en.

app for "collecting the wisdom of humanity."[2] StoryCorps has recorded more than 60,000 stories from more than 100,000 participants, some of which millions of listeners hear each week on NPR's *Morning Edition.*[3]

That's the connecting power of story. The first step in transformation is creating the *story* of your digital journey and making it one in which everyone can participate.

STORYTELLING:
OUR BRAINS ARE WIRED TO CONNECT

Language is the architecture of our daily lives. It is the medium of thought and how we express our ideas. With it we effect thousands of, well, achievements, including: creating relationships, making sense of our world, describing problems, and enlisting others to collaborate with us to generate innovative solutions. Within any organization, language equips us with effective ways to communicate intent, develop understanding, and coordinate action — which we do through the stories we tell.

Neuroscience suggests that people respond viscerally to stories, often altering their point of view or behaviors. One Princeton study showed, for example, a "mind meld" between a storyteller and listeners, causing both the producers and the consumers of the story to have similar brain activity. The authors suggest that this neural coupling may also be present during general conversation. "The stronger the coupling between the speaker and the listener's brain responses, the better the understanding," says researcher Uri

---

2 StoryCorps, "About StoryCorps," accessed May 19, 2017, https://storycorps.org/about/.

3 StoryCorps, "Frequently Asked Questions," accessed May 19, 2017, https://storycorps.org/faq/.

Hasson. "Sometimes when you speak with someone, you get the feeling that you cannot get through to them, and other times you know that you click. When you really understand each other, your brains become more similar in responses over time."[4]

But what does this have to do with digital transformation?

Confronted with evidence that opposes their beliefs, people, especially highly analytical people, quickly find 'data' that confirms their opinion. This *confirmation bias* is one of the most powerful ways we humans maintain our mental models and resist change. To influence others, to change their minds and actions, we must find common ground, something that we all agree about, and use this to create synchronization. This is one of the primary cause and effect roles of storytelling.

When you attempt to alter someone's beliefs and actions, you are exerting control over them—something people struggle to accept. *Using story to enroll people in the digital journey* expands their sense of control and increases their motivation and compliance.[5] What's more, as the listener synchronizes with the storyteller, their brain translates the story into a physical experience; we literally feel the emotions of the speaker. By physically and neurologically sharing their emotional state (empathy at its best), we begin to anticipate and predict what comes next in their story. This deepens our understanding and their influence over our behavior—literally embedding the change narrative in the listener.

As we synchronize with others, we are looking to them to

---

4 Ushma Patel, "Hasson Brings Real Life into the Lab to Examine Cognitive Processing," Princeton University, December 5, 2011, https://www.princeton.edu/main/news/archive/S32/27/76E76/index.xml?section=featured.

5 Tali Sharot, *The Influential Mind: What the Brain Reveals about our Power to Change Others.* (New York, NY: Henry Holt and Company, 2017).

fill the gaps in our knowledge and understanding, particularly during times of uncertainty or threat. During periods of transformation, our brains are on high alert for cues that suggest risk or danger—cues like changes to roles or responsibilities. The most accurate cues, we assume, come from those with the most complete and relevant information, the narrative provided by managers and leaders. To make their stories impactful, getting people to really listen, these narrators must highlight the information gap of their listeners (what they don't know but want to know) and fill it with positive, action oriented choices they can make. Making a choice is a neurological reward in itself (releasing the pleasure neurotransmitter dopamine), and we can build on this by encouraging the listener to contribute to the design or outcome the story seeks to achieve.

SOCIAL MEMES:
HARNESSING THE EMOTIONAL SPARK OF PEOPLE

But what have social memes to do with our storytelling? Like the genes they were named for, social memes are ideas, behaviors, speech, gestures, or rituals that convey meaning and, most importantly, can be culturally transmitted.[6] Memes arise from stories and are cues that trigger behaviors and ideas embedded in the narrative. They work by providing feedback on how people's behavior will be viewed by others. These cues are meaningful to us because our brains are designed to be influenced by others, to mimic their behaviors, beliefs, and values.[7] For example, a powerful organizational

---

6 Sandra Waddock, *Reflections: Intellectual Shamans, Sensemaking, and Memes in Large System Change*, Journal of Change Management, 15:4, 259-273, 2015.

7 Matthew Lieberman, *Social: Why Our Brains Are Wired to Connect*. (New York, NY: Crown Publishers, 2013).

meme is the *not invented here* meme, which produces resistance to new or external ideas. During digital transformation new memes are introduced, memes such as: rituals (iterative planning, backlog creation and refinement, and retrospectives); behaviors (an emphasis on learning, experimentation, and customer experience); and practices (writing user stories, designing end-to-end products, and cocreating features with the end user). Seeing or hearing others adopt new ideas and behaviors is a strong motivator of change, especially during times of uncertainty.

Memes about the digital transformation, and the stories that generate them, spread information between groups that normally don't exchange opinions or ideas, acting like social breadcrumbs and increasing the opportunity for social learning and adoption of new behaviors. Also like their genetic brethren, social memes have the ability to mutate, change, and recombine with other memes, even compete with existing memes, which is how they can change beliefs and, more specifically, corporate culture. Similarly memes can be inherited, or passed along to others in the company, but their most powerful form of biomimicry is their ability to self-replicate. This means that, once established, memes often maintain themselves until they evolve — impacted by new stories, new memes.

Perhaps the biggest storytelling challenge of any organizational transformation is this: The transformation story will typically take place in the context of a disengaged,[8] often change-fatigued workforce. In this case, developing a compelling story and then telling it repeatedly sets the stage for reengagement and

---

8 We make this assumption based on the Gallop engagement surveys from the last few years. For more information see: http://news.gallup.com/poll/188144/employee-engagement-stagnant-2015.aspx

participation. But how do you know that your story is achieving what you intend?

Companies undergoing digital transformation often ask for stories of how other companies have made the digital journey, and of course that is helpful, but the stories of other companies are never as moving as the story of you and your company. Regardless of your level or role in the transformation, people want to know what *you* think and how *you* feel. Then they want to contribute, to see their fingerprints on the plan. They want their inputs taken seriously. In short, people need to see *themselves* as characters in the company's transformation narrative.

Understandably, this can create a highly charged — and sometimes uncomfortable — space for leaders and change agents. Transformational leaders must be willing to be vulnerable, to provide direction even while not knowing all the answers . . . qualities rarely practiced or rewarded in corporate life. Yet those very acts of courage and authenticity, captured in stories, are at the heart of all transformation, and such acts are the reason the people who attempt large-scale transformation succeed.

Culture, memes, social physics, and the interactions among people, roles, and groups[9] — all these make up the social fabric of the enterprise and represent an enormous asset . . . or a potential liability. If you activate, align, and mobilize this social fabric, it becomes an asset; but if you fail to complete these tasks, this same social fabric will restrict the speed and effectiveness of your movement through each digital wave. Both informal social networks and collaborative communities support and transmit the

---

9 Alex Pentland, *Social Physics: How Social Networks Can Make Us Smarter*, reissue ed. (New York: Penguin Books, 2015); Etienne, Wenger, *Communities of Practice: Learning, Meaning, and Identity*, (Cambridge, MA: Cambridge University Press, 1999).

stories of transformation. They enlist the knowledge, talent, and interest of everyone in even a huge, sprawling corporation. They center people on a purpose about which they are passionate — maybe it's DevOps, a specific infrastructure, a platform challenge, a customer segment, or a corporate strategy. As automation creates more time in people's calendars, community becomes a bigger part of every workday, able to inform and speed up your digital transformation.

Corporate communities are particularly important in geographically dispersed companies; they are hotbeds of information flow, producing learning and places of belonging and contribution. Communities operate as social labs, where people come up with new ways of working together, provide feedback to change agents, and, ultimately, change their own behaviors and mindsets. When change gets scary, they provide support, helping us to interpret situations and to decide how to respond. Moving through the digital waves, such communities become the practice field for self-management, self-governance, and self-organization, and they create the norms for how people apply these across the company.

Netflix has a great story of community,[10] one it uses to maintain a positive culture and its corporate identity. Even more impressive is the personal narrative we heard recently over lunch from one of its senior technology leaders. As she described corporate events, shared ideas, encouraged discussion, and gave out business cards emblazoned with movie characters (ours had King Julien from *Madagascar*), she conveyed her story about working at Netflix and confirmed the corporate narrative and values: inclusion, trust, teaming, engagement, participatory leadership, diversity, pride, and ambition. Her

---

10   Reed Hastings, "Culture," SlideShare, August 1, 2009, https://www.slideshare.net/reed2001/culture-1798664.

story said more about the company and its values than any case study could ever capture.

Contrast this with other enterprises we work with whose leaders and employees openly admit their reluctance to identify their employer at social gatherings so that they don't have to listen to endless complaints! The internal narrative at companies like these are produced by memes of authority, keeping your head down, fear of speaking up, and lack of individual power. The story and, by extension, the culture of these companies is unbalanced and teetering, and a digital transformation could easily tip them into oblivion.

LANGUAGE TO CHANGE MINDSET AND IMPROVE ENGAGEMENT

So what is it we need to talk about — and in what ways — during digital transformation? From one wave to the next, the technical work becomes increasingly complex and abstract, while the adaptive work needs to become more concrete and personal. As digital technologies build on each other, each wave also requires more nontechnical organizational stakeholders — business partners, sales and marketing, and customers — to participate. Because of this it is critical to differentiate between the *technical* and *adaptive* challenges and opportunities you face as you make the transformation journey.

Digital transformation that simply focuses on technical change ignores the very factors required for it to succeed — an emphasis on people and the organization's operating model and culture. For technical transformation to succeed, leaders must identify and resolve adaptive challenges, causing the organization to evolve and become aligned with the emerging technology in each of the digital waves (recall the Digital Wave Model in Chapter 2). To achieve this, organizations must define and use both technical and adaptive language appropriate for each wave as they navigate the digital journey.

Technical language is used for physical or digital problems, hypotheses, and solutions; it may refer to code, infrastructure, or processes. Because data is also language, technical language can further describe analytical insights, trends, and quantitative knowledge. A large enterprise will move through the digital waves as distinct groups, using many "dialects" of data. These dialects—such as analytics, algorithms, financial results, and so on—occur throughout the company, providing common ground for communication between those who know the language. As one author noted: "The language of data is, like any other language, a social construct, and [requires] social norms around [it] to ensure not just clear communication but organizational cohesion."[11]

In contrast to technical language, *adaptive language* describes social, interpersonal, and organizational challenges and opportunities. It solves human and organizational problems and shapes the environment so that technical solutions can emerge. Just as digital teams must constantly remove technical debt from their solutions to improve quality, we must also identify and remove *social debt* from our interactions to ensure collaboration and cooperation. During transformation, there are two critical adaptive patterns that companies must learn to use: working *on* the organization and working *in* the organization.

Working *on* the organization uncovers stories and memes that

---

11 "Lessons from Becoming a Data-Driven Organization," *MIT Sloan Management Review*, October 18, 2016, http://sloanreview.mit.edu/case-study/lessons-from-becoming-a-data-driven-organization/.

are amplifying or limiting people's ability to change or learn. As you listen to people talk about the digital transformation, you will hear the stories and memes that are spreading across the social networks within your company. Limiting memes are often entrenched unquestioned assumptions that produce rigid ideas and behaviors and reinforce the clay layer that forms in the middle of many companies. But adaptive language can reverse these by creating new memes and stories that provide the organization with the means to structure communities; transfer learning, insights, and ideas across boundaries; shape points of view; and create common meaning and collective understanding. As a result, adaptive language helps us map the workplace so that we can find ways to fit in, participate, and contribute. Memes and stories that communicate the collective work *on* the organization produce the organizational culture we experience daily.

Working *in* the organization relies on technical language but also needs adaptive language to provide for reflection and feedback. Using adaptive language while working *in* the organization avoids creating accidental adversaries, reinforces new memes and norms, and promotes collaboration. These types of feedback loops are prerequisites for complex technical solutions and social coordination, both of which are crucial in the digital landscape. For example, we might find while working *in* the organization that we need better teaming, information flow, or integration of ideas across boundaries. In such cases, working *in* the organization informs us about the need to work *on* the organization.

WORDS CREATE WORLDS

Language is neurologically hardwired and structures our ideas and thoughts. This means that the words people hear daily influence their view of the world and their interactions with it. Words can create, limit, or expand our perceptions, often allowing a novel idea to emerge and develop from an abstract concept into a concrete reality. To achieve this we use our brain's ability to imagine and predict what others are thinking, a process called "mentalizing" or Theory of Mind.[12]

Mentalizing enables us to consider the thoughts and reactions of others as we interact with them. This ensures that we are, and remain, part of the tribe (inclusion and belonging) and it increases the social rewards that matter to us (being connected, treated fairly, praised, and respected). In fact, the natural 'resting' state of the brain, times when we are not focused on task work, is being socially attuned. This means that even casually watching the interpersonal interactions of others causes us to imagine and interpret what they are thinking—we make a story of why they are behaving the way they are. It is the readiness to think socially that we want to take advantage of during transformation.

During periods of uncertainty, change, and developing new relationships (frequently a side effect of transformation) our success, or failure, in achieving the outcomes we want depends on our ability to predict the mental state of others, what they are thinking and feeling. Digital transformation shifts the emphasis from working as individual contributors or in silos (functional, business, or technical) to working collectively on teams, collaborating with others we are not familiar with, and coordinating complex work across organizational boundaries. These are all activities that require mentalizing, and mentalizing takes effort. Research finds that most of us underutilize our ability to understand and connect with our colleagues at work. In other words, we don't take

---

12 Matthew Lieberman, *Social: Why Our Brains Are Wired to Connect.* (New York, NY: Crown Publishers, 2013).

full advantage of the natural abilities of our brains, abilities we all have had all our lives.

Our ability to imagine and predict what others are thinking and how they may respond is critical to our ability to shape and share information, be it a technical request or an adaptive story of how a collective decision was made. From the moment we take in information, our brain begins to consider whom we could share this with and how to shape it to make it compelling for the listener. This ensures that our listener understands our words the way we intend them.

Thus, even in the digital world, the old adage "Talk is cheap" is patently wrong. In fact, talk is extremely valuable, and miscommunication can be very expensive. If you don't understand what others mean or your point of view is rejected, talk can become very pricey. When large organizations composed of thousands of intelligent and diverse people haven't learned how to shape conversations — or to influence and engage people through stories — their ability to transform is hindered and often stalls. In a world focused on apps and tools, having the ability to inspire and direct our actions and to nourish our will through conversation is key to a successful digital transformation.

Investing in creating a *collective* story and sharing information via language, memes, and individual stories avoids the common scenario where people create their own version of what is happening and begin making decisions and acting based on a fabricated version of reality — which can become a meme and story of its own, derailing your transformation. How people interpret your words or interactions (even if they are merely observers) is critical to how they make sense of the transformation and triggers perceptions — both positive and negative — about how it impacts them.

Through story, your words produce behaviors and beliefs that spread throughout the organization as memes. The story of transformation begins to make sense, amplifying positive feelings, dampening negative feelings, and motivating people to participate and take ownership of outcomes. Stories give us the means to *intentionally* design our transformational journey. Through them we articulate ideas of all kinds and solve a vast array of problems. Social learning shapes and makes sense of data and information, enriches social interactions, and infuses transformation with human bonding.

Because stories are potent initiators of the digital transformation and establish a set of memes for the groundswell of corporate change, we need a framework to hold the story of the transformation — a container for alignment, coordination, and ambition. Next, we explore an iterative cycle of transformation that uses our transformational language, memes, and social physics.

SOCIAL MEMES RECAP

How we talk to ourselves and others creates the content of the transformational narrative. That's why it's so important to use clearly defined words and concepts to create a positive, inclusive environment. Memes help close the information gap and reduce confusion that arises when people in authority use vague language. Words define the new and differentiate it from the old, providing clarity and purpose to questions like: What are we jettisoning and why? Stories of transformation define and translate corporate strategies and goals into something everyone can understand, pass on, and adhere to. Positive personal stories fill the narrative space that people constantly engage in, crowding out rumors and unproductive dialogue. In short, capturing the journey in a story makes the experience of transformation *real* for people.

KEY TAKEAWAYS: SOCIAL MEMES
(BY POSITION WITHIN AN ORGANIZATION)

Executives:

Recognize the impact you have on others and make it intentional. Get feedback: Realize the we all have blind spots, and address these. Become an observer, learn to spot verbal, visual, and social cues, and adapt your language and expressions to get the outcomes you want. Set the context for sensemaking and be available (open, interested, and present); prepare ahead of time, then act in the moment and focus on your listeners rather than yourself. Avoid hidden agendas, be truthful, and expect people to respond as adults, partners, and equals in achieving the goals you've set.

Transformation Leaders:

Constantly be on the lookout and observe what works and what doesn't during your social interactions. Remember that you are a highly visible role model and are always being observed. Be aware of the intention and objectives you are trying to communicate, watch and ask for feedback, and adjust as you go. Use unstructured, creative forms of interaction, like stories and metaphor, to present your ideas and to leave space for the listener to provide input. Avoid *role-speak* and the use of jargon or technical-only language, remembering that the biggest challenges and opportunities are adaptive. Accept people for where they are at the moment; people who are frustrated and fearful one minute can become excited and bold the next.

Managers:

Your people are just learning new behaviors and skills; avoid criticizing, disputing, arguing, and negativity. To coach, or correct course, use active listening and inquiry, and recognize any and all wins people are achieving. To become more other-focused try our Con-nect~Engage~Act interaction format: *Connect* to get people's atten-tion and make it both personal and safe before you make your case; *Engage* to cocreate the interaction (rather than making it one-way only) by using metaphor, narrative, zooming in and out, drawing, mapping, and playing with ideas; *Act* by staying focused on learning, advances, outcomes, and results.

Employees:

Write a personal mission statement: How do you want others to experience you? Stay focused on opportunities and possibilities. Pick a few words you want others to associate with you and your contri-butions, words like positive, energetic, thoughtful, inclusive, inter-esting, etc. — and focus on *living* these every day.

Abe drums his fingers on the table. Gina said she would join him for lunch to explain how she accomplished transformation without losing people in the process. So far, that seemed the one area in which Abe had become proficient: losing people along the way — especially when he tried to explain the *how* of the transformation he had in mind. He could explain his vision and tell the story of corporate transformation, but he couldn't seem to develop a good way of explaining how the company would achieve this. He was hearing people use the language of working *in* and *on* the organization; in fact, someone had asked him yesterday if what he was proposing was more an *adaptive* challenge than a *technical* opportunity. But then they would ask: "What should we start doing tomorrow? I mean, is there a plan, or do we just start experimenting? How do we know if we are going in the right direction?"

As he thinks about these things, Abe still smiles to himself. In the month since he had last seen Gina, he had achieved a lot; his own personal transformation was in high gear. The only thing he seemed to be struggling with was describing the process that he wanted people to use to achieve their digital transformation; unfortunately, this was one place he couldn't afford to come up short. If people didn't know how to act, what to actually *do*, they would do nothing!

"There you are!" Gina says, interrupting Abe's reverie and breezily giving him a hug before settling herself at the table. "What's so urgent? And how can I help?"

"I need a crash course on how to explain transformation!" Abe blurts out. "So far all I seem to have created is confusion. I'm getting buy-in, but I don't know how to tell everyone exactly *what* we are doing, let alone how we are going to do it . . . and what I want each of them, specifically, to do. You've done this. You've led a successful transformation. You were able to include both technology and the business . . . What did you do? And how?"

Gina throws her head back and laughs. "Oh, Abe, I felt just like that! So many times and so many days I thought I was the herald of confusion!"

"So what did you do?"

"I did what you're doing—I looked for help. And I found it. A friend gave me a framework that had *just enough structure* . . . her words. Let's order, and I'll tell you what she told me. And calm down, it works like a charm."

With lunch on its way, Gina launches into her story. "First of all, this is not about technology. It is about people, including customers . . . which means it is about business. When your business partners see only your fancy technology, bells and whistles, it is hard to frame the digital transformation correctly. I presented the transformation to my business partners as a customer-focused play, not a technical upgrade. That meant that we had to integrate *the work of business into* the work of technology. On the tech side, we had to begin to understand what our customers wanted, and we had to focus on products, not features or projects. On the business side, my partners had to move away from funding projects and widgets, and away from waterfall and burdensome requirements documentation. It meant new skills and processes on their side as well as ours, new ways of working *with* us, not us working *for* them. These were huge steps for us. In most cases, we were looking at the need to reorg, and I worried that these steps would stop our transformation before we even started."

"Boy, I can totally understand that," Abe agrees. "We don't have the best relationship with our business partners, and as technologists we suffer from a sort of 'shiny new object syndrome.' To have even a chance at success, I need a way to make this change action-able for my business partners *and* the technology organization."

"Right," responds Gina. "First, *start where you are* and then *follow yes.* Let me break this down for you."

Gina takes out a piece of paper and creates a chart. Together Abe and Gina fill out the chart, capturing the challenges and opportunities they each see as part of the transformation. When they finish, Gina sits back and her thoughts seem to capture all of her attention for a moment. Abe watches patiently, but he thinks, 'Gina has just provided me with a framework that I can use to explain this process to the whole organization!'

"The hard part, Abe," Gina says, coming back into the conversation, "is that you are not really following a prescribed path; you can't simply create a road map and place it on every desk. That was our old world. In this new world, we want a more dynamic transformation, one where you — and everyone with you — *learn(s) as you go. That's* what 'the edge of chaos' means. One day it is too stable and needs disruption and innovation, the next it's too chaotic and needs leadership and structure. And the tricky part is that the need to *work on and in* the organization is constantly shifting as the ecosystem evolves. At your level, when you are looking at the whole company, everything is in motion. I remember thinking I was watching molecules of change bouncing around like molecules of water in my high school science class. It can be very disquieting, yes, even disruptive, especially for you and other leaders. But you can't control it, yet you can't just sit still and do nothing. You have to poke it, probe it, disrupt it, and let the ecosystem respond, then settle down so it can get ready for the next experiment. Make sense?"

"Viscerally, yes; intellectually, no," Abe responds. "Is there *any* way to design or plan these pokes, probes, and experiments?"

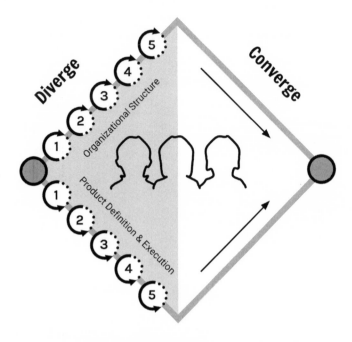

Figure I.1. **The graphic Gina draws for Abe.**

Gina takes out another sheet of paper and draws a large diamond on it (Figure I.1). "The key, Abe, is that you work *on and in* the organization simultaneously. Think of the upper part of this diamond as working *on* the organization and the lower part as working *in* the organization. And the four corners provide you with key pivot points: Horizontally they are takeoff and landing points, places where you can pivot and correct course; vertically they are where you shift from diverging and exploring to converging and coming to consensus.

"I typically use a two-week sprint cadence. The first week is all design and innovation, and the second operational and outcome focused. The process lets you work simultaneously on technical issues, maybe a product or adoption of a new tool, and also the adaptive issues they produce, like the customer experience of the product or the impact of the new tool on operations. This gives people *just enough structure* to chunk the transformation and work on it a slice at a time. It's as 'easy' as that!"

Their business lunch completed, Abe walks back to his office on a high note. He may not know exactly *what* to do, but, after his time with Gina, he has a good idea of *how* to operationalize his transformation. More importantly, he feels that his main concern has been addressed: He knows this process can engage and involve everyone in the company.

Chapter 6

Helix Cycles — Operationalize Continuous Transformation

Let's visit a large financial institution that has been on a technically focused agile journey for the last four years. We will call the company CreditCentral. Recently, they have engaged their business partners with a bold proposition: Work with us to reinvent IT, to modernize it and become customer and product focused.

With the top executives on board, many business partners are lined up and ready to take the journey. They are asking, "How do we shift *from* our process-heavy, tightly managed project world *to* value creation delivered by loosely coupled, autonomous teams of multi-skilled business and technology experts?" In other words: "How do we simultaneously work both *in and on* our business (end-to-end product development and organizational transformation) and, by default, the entire corporation?"

CreditCentral faces the same challenges that most large

corporations in almost all industries face today: taking advantage of the digital revolution without stumbling, and transforming the organization, while moving at warp speed, without damaging their reputation or customer relations, depleting their coffers and talent, and slowing their value creation and market share. To better understand how to work through these challenges, let's take a quick walk back in time to another era, one in many ways quite like today.

In 1993, with IBM on the brink of disaster, Lou Gerstner took over the helm. In his book *Who Says Elephants Can't Dance?*[1] Gerstner states that he took on the challenge of saving and transforming the company because the demise of IBM, he felt, would have social and national repercussions beyond simple economics. We feel that the same situation exists today with many large global enterprises: They aren't too large to fail, but rather are *economically too important* to be allowed to fail. Faced with the transformation to digital, this sentiment exists within the executive ranks of CreditCentral.

Oddly, Gerstner also stated that he had no preconceived notion of what was needed for the survival and transformation of IBM. Sound like a bad situation? Not at all. By this point it should be clear: This mindset, though mostly lacking in business today, is one that all leaders of the digital transformation need to adopt! Embrace the fact that your transformation can't be planned and rolled out, top-down, as you did pre-digital.

As IBM's CEO, Gerstner offered no special protection to any person, group, or product; no matter how successful they had been in the past, no person or group would be exempt from scrutiny

---

1 Louis V. Gerstner, Jr. *Who Says Elephants Can't Dance?: Leading A Great Enterprise Through Dramatic Change. (New York, NY: HarperBusiness, 2003).*

and change. This is also required today. As they begin their digital transformation, many large enterprises struggle because they love their infrastructure, architecture, bureaucracy, processes, and procedures. At CreditCentral an 18-step, seven-plus-month project approval and funding process has their business and technology teams twisted in knots and managing spreadsheets rather than creating customer value. How can they be expected to simply trash all of that?

Organizationally, Gerstner acted quickly to eliminate bureaucracy, replacing it with a balanced, decentralized decision-making process aligned to a customer-focused strategy, which he called Operation Bear Hug. He asked every business leader to rethink what they were doing, as well as to determine why — and how — they were going to rapidly transform their business. He also took a bold step and mandated that, if and where it was needed, rightsizing had to be done quickly and fairly.[2] Contrast this with CreditCentral, where an operations group (3,000 people globally) is being asked to eliminate themselves over five years, to be replaced by an automated technology platform. The result? Executives are focused on yearly headcount reduction to make their cost-saving numbers, regardless of the status of the replacement platform, and teams are so fearful of losing their jobs that they battle each other and are unable to deliver an operating model that could achieve a successful future state.

IBM had built their reputation on offering customers comprehensive solutions and support, and Gerstner knew that he couldn't sacrifice this. He emphasized the customer experience and insisted that IBM continue to offer whole solutions that addressed the emerging software-based market ecosystem — even

---

2 Ibid.

if it meant continuing to support their antiquated mainframe business for a time. This is the same type of challenge Credit-Central faces today: Their digital solutions must be omnichannel, delivered where, when, and how the customer wants to inter-act with their money, credit cards, auto loans, investments, and home mortgages. CreditCentral must provide a seamless expe-rience that puts control of the customer's life in the customer's hands, whether that customer is an individual, a business owner, or a large corporation.

Gerstner attacked transforming his company on all fronts simul-taneously rather than slowly and sequentially. He made changes throughout the organization. IBM would often have more than 100 transformational change programs functioning at any one time. From 1994 to 1998, this level of reengineering saved $9.5 billion, with $14 billion in overall savings.[3]

We now know that Gerstner's ideas brought IBM back from the verge of collapse, though, at the time, it seemed no better chance than a coin flip. When he became CEO in the early 1990s, there were 128 CIOs in the company, each with their own local systems architecture and homegrown apps! When Gerstner retired in 2002, there was one CIO. By the end of 1995, two short years after he had arrived, IBM had saved $2 billion in IT expenses and had gone from 155 datacenters down to 16. Over this period IBM consolidated 31 internal communication networks into one, providing the ability to coordinate work across business silos and regions. Delivery of business value also improved dramatically; hardware development was reduced from four years to 16 months or less, and on-time product delivery increased from 30 percent to 95 percent.[4]

---

3 Ibid.

4 Ibid.

That was IBM. But how about CreditCentral? And how about today? How might they manage their digital transformation? Are there lessons from the past that we can mashup with the current digital challenges to create a repeatable, reliable way to move through the waves? There is. We call it "Helix."

FROM POSSIBILITIES TO DECISIONS: DYNAMIC LEARNING CYCLES

Helix is the *how* of digital transformation. This is a system designed to work both *on* the company and *in* the market, adaptively shaping the organization while delivering value to customers. Helix equips middle managers with new ways to contribute and the product team with the means to collaborate with legal, compliance/risk, HR, and regulatory colleagues. It achieves this by bringing diverse points of view, needs, and outcomes into creative tension, then resolving that tension using an iterative learning process: sense-test-adapt (see sidebar).

The framework also provides a structure for two-way conversations — between business and technology, between the product team and customers, and among multiple functional teams across the company. These conversations create new behaviors, ways of working collaboratively, and the means of establishing continuous feedback and flow of information. The Helix framework builds cocreation and learning into the company's daily operating rhythm, orchestrating the transformation at an enterprise level. This is how the enterprise overcomes the pain of digital transformation. Unlike manufactured products, digital products and services can be rapidly changed, updated, and innovated. This generates opportunity . . . but also problems. While the ability to continuously innovate creates the prospect of learning from customers how *they* want to use your product, it also introduces uncertainty into the product development cycle, a difficulty experienced by most large companies.

Enter the Sense-Test-Adapt learning cycle.

Sense-Test-Adapt is built into the Helix framework using two-vectors: a *divergent*, exploratory phase, followed by a *convergent*, implementation phase (Figure 6.1.).

SENSE-TEST-ADAPT LEARNING CYCLE

Sense: Sensing starts with an idea, a vision for a product or service. It assumes that there is much you don't know about the market, customer, or need for your idea. By establishing a two-way conversation with the customer or end user, you begin to understand their needs and how they might use your idea, product, or service to satisfy their goals. This conversation can take many forms: customer journey maps, jobs to be done, qualitative research, traditional market research, or digital data collection and analytics. Key to this phase of the cycle is using design thinking to define and expand the problem space before any solutions are discussed.

Test: With a robust problem space, numerous solutions (or partial solutions) can be identified and tested in the marketplace. In this phase, experiments, with a complete set of assumptions and hypotheses, reduce uncertainty and risk, and product teams learn by doing. Experiments run typically no more than 3-5 days using bare bones, low-risk methods. Testing provides the opportunity to refine and enrich your product.

Adapt: Adaptation applies learning in the form of new ideas, experiences, and features. Progress is measured as the reduction of uncertainty as the team works through their backlog of questions, assumptions, and hypotheses to generate customer value.

The divergent phase begins from a common understanding of what the product team intends to accomplish during the Helix cycle, the ideas, questions, and assumptions they are exploring. The diverging vectors enable the product team to resolve the creative tension between, for example, customer and product, technical and adaptive, working on and in the organization, or balancing business and customer values. Breaking into two sides, the team intentionally designs short hypothesis-driven experiments to generate learning in both directions; for example: exploring the addition of a new functionality with customers *and* technically resolving a previously determined pain point in the customer experience.

The second phase of the Helix cycle, convergence, is outcome focused. This phase begins with the product team's reviewing the learning generated by their divergent work. Synthesizing and identifying what is feasible, desirable, and viable enables the product team to make decisions, plan their execution, and deliver epics and features for the new functionality to the development teams. The conclusion of the convergence phase is the integration of the organizational or customer oriented work into the product backlog. This clears the way for the product team to focus on the next Helix cycle of learning while development teams build, test, and deploy new functionality.

The Helix cycle establishes a culture of exploration and experimentation while also providing *clean fuel* to agile teams. Clean fuel focuses on customer and business outcomes, not delivered features or outputs. At its simplest, clean fuel comprises the activities that provide information and feedback necessary for agile teams to do their best work. Although this sounds standard for technology companies, the integration of business, technology, and customers creates a challenge for most enterprises. As product teams mature and

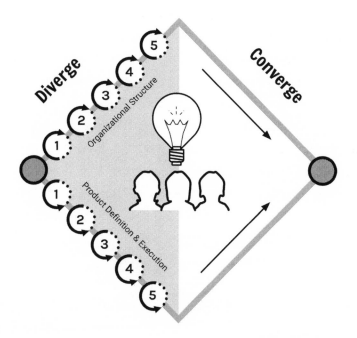

Figure 6.1. **Helix is an iterative cycle that simultaneously works in two complimentary directions applying the sense-test-adapt process.**

advance through the waves, clean fuel evolves, reducing barriers, becoming more strategic, and applying end-to-end approaches to product development.

The dual vector process provides a pragmatic and actionable way to operationalize business strategy with the product team taking responsibility and ownership for market opportunities and challenges. Using Helix and working a couple of sprints ahead of agile teams, the product team can adjust their strategy and cocreate with customers without slowing throughput. Ultimately, Helix produces a disciplined way of integrating business and technology that amplifies everyone's ability to respond, learn, and innovate together.

HELIX:
ITERATIVE TRANSFORMATION IN ACTION

Helix enables digital transformation by increasing the responsiveness of the organization to demands for change based on the needs
of products and customers. The framework is ultralightweight and
intended to provide just enough structure for the product team to
tackle problems that were once only in the purview of corporate
change management, external consultants, or digital natives.

There are three phases to the Helix cycle: the Takeoff Point, the
Midpoint, and the Landing Point. Helix can be used as a single cycle
of change that addresses an opportunity or challenge (Figure 6.1),
or multiple cycles can be strung together to accomplish broader,
more significant transformation (Figure 6.2). When strung together,
Helix cycles can be aligned to technical sprints, allowing the product team to deliver requirements strategically and in small batches
without excessive documentation.

Takeoff Point (Establishing Outcomes and Gaining Momentum): The takeoff

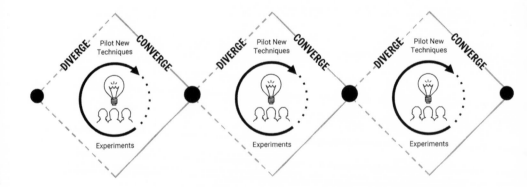

Figure 6.2. **Iterative Helix cycles allow product teams to continuously
adapt their organization and workflow to enable innovation and technical advance.**

point creates common ground for the diverse product team. Common ground is established using a workshop or a working session format and produces the activities, experiments, and collaboration that will take place during the divergent phase. Finally, the product team will split into two groups: one working to advance organizational, adaptive, outside-in work, and the other to advance product, technical, inside-out work. Both vectors generate customer and business value.

The takeoff point is where the product team identifies and clarifies one or two experiments for the Helix cycle (Figure 6.3). These are based on learning from the previous cycle and new customer insights or feedback, and they create a continuous flow of product discovery and innovation. For example, a product team may identify a desired outcome from the last cycle's work with customers. This generates multiple opportunities, assumptions, and hypotheses on how to technically solution it—each of which can be explored and tested using short, well-defined experiments during the first week of the Helix cycle.

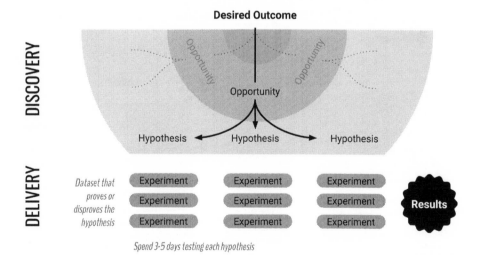

Figure 6.3: **The Helix framework establishes experiments that the product team uses to explore value creating work.**

Good experiments place the product team at the boundary of knowing and not knowing, exploring the space between what they can and cannot do. The practice of good experimentation follows a distinctive pattern: First, a few desired outcomes are chosen; these serve as short-term targets. Next, each three- to five-day experiment tests a clearly stated hypothesis using metrics that define success and failure, and each may be adaptive, "Will the customer respond favorably to this outcome?" or technical, "Can we build this given our existing architecture?" Experiments can be thought experiments, customer experience mapping, prototypes, in-market A/B testing, technical evaluations . . . or any number of processes; the sky's the limit. What's important is that experiments are intentional, well designed, and have clear metrics that can be interpreted and acted upon.

To generate the experiments, we recommend the use of a learning canvas to assist the product team in turning reality and real-time data into hypotheses and experiments that can be tested. Action-Insight Mapping (AIM) (Figure 6.4) is a quick and easy way to bring the diverse members of the product team together to collectively learn and design each upcoming Helix cycle.[5]

Once the experiments are set, the product team assigns themselves to either vector. Within each vector, the team is free to structure their work as they please. The composition of the two groups can vary between Helix cycles, and the team can recruit people from outside the product team for their expertise, experience, or insights.

---

5 This learning canvas is adapted from two processes: (1) After Action Review and (2) "Growing Knowledge Together: Using Emergent Learning and EL Maps for Better Results." Marilyn Darling and Charles Perry in *Reflections, The SoL Journal, Volume 8, No 1, 2007.*

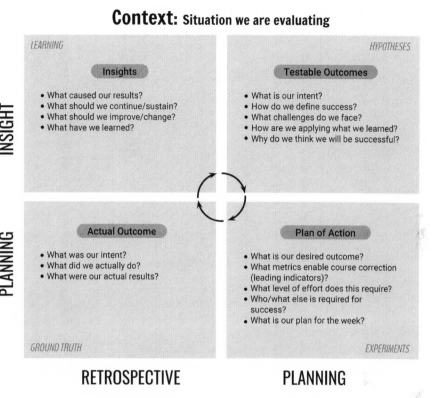

Figure 6.4. **Action-Insight Mapping is a quick way to harvest learning from the past and generate experiments for the next Helix cycle.**

Midpoint (The Point of Maximum Divergence and Initiation of Convergence): Of course you can't experiment forever. We find that the reason many companies dislike the idea of experimenting and are reluctant to incorporate it into product development is that their poor hypotheses formation and testing make the effort seem not only tedious, but useless. This knowledge gap robs product teams of the ability to create customer and business value. Better hypotheses creation and validation produce well-designed experiments that produce often unexpected information that can be acted upon during the next phase of the cycle.

At the midpoint of the Helix cycle the product groups come back together, report their findings, and make decisions and recommendations that they can take forward into the convergence phase of the cycle. What have our experiments and explorations revealed? How do we turn this learning into action? Again, the AIM canvas supports the development of outcomes for the action phase of the Helix cycle.

Following the midpoint, the convergence phase brings the two vectors back together. This phase is typically when the product team gains input from the development teams on their recommendations, updates senior leadership, and acts on the decisions they have made.

For example, a global team at CreditCentral spent multiple Helix sprints (Figure 6.2) integrating their modern digital platform (technology transformation) into their middle office operating model (organizational transformation). Because the five regional offices had different national, legal, and regulatory requirements, each phase of convergence included market-specific adjustments to their go-forward plan. The Helix diverge-converge cycle enabled them to collectively be bold and think creatively while ensuring compliance with regional regulations.

Landing Point (Anchoring Decisions and Informing Others): Convergence ends at a single point, ensuring alignment and establishing new common ground to push off from for the next Helix cycle. The two teams come together and share their results and accomplishments, what they've learned and challenges they've faced. The landing point is usually a working session that brings all key stakeholders together for transparency, cross-pollination, reduction of risk and dependencies, collaboration and cooperation, and learning. This makes it useful to include the next Takeoff Point as the second half of the session. The landing point concludes the Helix cycle with reflection (Figure 6.5), maturing the product team as they work together.

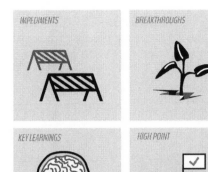

Reflection

1. What *impediments* did we encounter?

2. What *breakthroughs* did we make?

3. What *key learnings* help us work better collectively?

4. What was my *personal high point* this week and why?

5. What next steps can we take to make *progress* as a team?

6. What *outcomes* do we expect these to produce?

Figure 6.5. **A regular reflection ceremony prior to planning the next Helix cycle improves the product team's ability to push the boundaries of their knowledge and blast through constraints and unquestioned assumptions to become a high performing team.**

For large, complex enterprises (socially, financially, and/or technically complex) Helix offers a way to address opportunities and challenges systemically, at their roots. With its multiple feedback loops, Helix provides the means for product teams to constantly and autonomously adjust their behaviors and actions based on new information. As we see in the next chapter, when Helix is used with Strive (a holistic performance management system) the company benefits from the interactions of many parts that, in concert, give rise to a whole new set of possibilities for growth.

CUSTOMER-CENTRIC, PRODUCT-BASED DEVELOPMENT

Perhaps *the* most important requirement of digital transformation is understanding your customer. The digital marketplace is constantly morphing and shifting, impacted by consumer expectations, digital natives, and new entrants. As digital natives proliferate, they establish a radically different customer experience. This move toward customer centricity is amplified by everyone's increasingly digital life.

Luckily, customers are excited and delighted. For example, they now compare their experience with banking to their experience with Amazon; more, they want to close the gap between what could formerly have been considered disparate processes.[6] To stay afloat, corporations must stop seeing IT as the department of automation and cost-cutting and start seeing digital transformation as the means of end-to-end value creation. This means rethinking the concept of projects and how businesses interact with customers.

Think of your digital transformation as a product revolution. Wave 0 and Wave 1 companies still use projects as the primary construct around which they mobilize, plan, fund, and deliver features or small pieces of work. Projects are snapshots in time, slivers of larger products that the business believes will produce value. They typically have an inside-out focus and concentrate on bits and pieces of products that someday may combine to produce customer value.

In contrast, products are long-lived, customer-centric and have important strategic implications. They imply investment and cross-organizational decision-making, prioritization, and trade-offs. Products require dedicated cross-disciplinary teams to collectively imagine and deliver value, creating a new organizational operating model. If we're going to pursue the idea of turning projects into

---

6 https://beta.theglobeandmail.com/report-on-business/rob-commentary/why-cant-my-bank-be-more-like-amazon/article35883327/?ref=https://www.theglobeandmail.com&service=mobile

products (see sidebar), we need to transform how we mobilize decision-making and distribute authority; but we must also reconsider the definition of "product" itself.

Decision-making for products is far more strategic than that required by project work. The long-lived, customer-centric nature of products requires decision makers to make choices continuously, outlining future possibilities as well as addressing immediate needs. Product development requires decision-makers to incorporate new learning, technology, and customer needs into the existing plan, making tradeoffs that require a depth of understanding that top executives lack. These highlight the need for authority to be localized and for decision-making to be timely and actionable.

Additionally, products typically include a wide group of diverse stakeholders, including customers. Nike+, for example, is a blend of clothing, running shoes, technology, and a third-party platform (Apple's iPod) all designed to work within an interactive customer ecosystem. Product development leaders are responsible for the convergence of customer use, technology, and product design — managing a blurred line between the physical and digital attributes of the product. For instance, products that were once only dealt with in the physical realm — like purchasing a new automobile through a car dealer — are now physical *and* digital: buying a car through a search and choice of many online retailers. It is obvious how much the end-to-end customer experience is radically changing.

Because it's not purely physical, but instead is software based, it's often difficult to see a product from the customer's perspective. This makes it easy to get trapped into thinking that a platform is a product or an app is a product. But to really define a product, you must begin with a customer, a customer with a

FROM PROJECTS TO PRODUCTS

The challenges of shifting from project to product approach are many:

First, projects are often built on the needs of software development and focus on components, ignoring the holistic way a customer uses the product.

Second, to succeed in the product space, you cannot focus only on the technology delivered; you must understand the customer and his experience using your product. End-to-end product development is rooted in the customer journey, the problems they are trying to solve and the outcomes they seek.

Third, the minute you step away from projects, with their mature operationalized processes that are deeply embedded into the corporate fabric, you come into conflict with additional processes and structures that have been in place, often for decades.

Fourth, as you start to think more holistically about the customer experience and the ways that customers seek value, you ask questions that involve the entire company. Now you're confronted with a very stark realization: To deliver customer value, new organizational structures, functionality, and relationships are needed.

problem. For example, consider the ability to apply online for a home mortgage: The customer doesn't need a mortgage; the customer needs a home. The mortgage is only part of the problem of buying a home, and the online solution is only part of the customer's experience. In all cases, to provide the greatest customer value your product needs to solve as much of the customer's problem as possible, ideally delivering a complete, end-to-end solution. This often means establishing an ecosystem of partners to address the entire customer journey, as, say, Nike and Apple did for their running communities.

Understanding and building for the entire customer journey requires an outside-in approach to product development. The more you solve the customer's whole problem, the more your product can address their whole experience. And this is where large enterprises can get creative and compete with the digital natives. Large enterprises have suites of products and services and can combine offerings, from multiple lines of business to making public internal tools and platforms.

This challenge — and *opportunity* — is what Helix is designed to address. For example, imagine a product team that is trying to incorporate digital into an existing, tangible product. Whirlpool did this for their refrigerators, Cooking Light magazine did it for their online offers, and GE and others are doing it for the Internet of Things. Or imagine commercializing your digital solutions. Amazon productized their cloud computing, creating Amazon Web Services (AWS). And from the same playbook, The Washington Post's *Arc* platform offers tools and content to the news industry. Facebook has launched *Workplace*, designed to connect the organization using their familiar tools. And Netflix has replaced DVDs with streaming video.

How might Helix help you achieve similar movement??

First Helix enables you to learn what kinds of digital product or service your existing customers would want and use — which, in turn, determines design, features, and where to invest your resources. Working with customers Helix identifies *what* problems, experiences, and outcomes they are seeking: what to build and what *not* to build. Simultaneously the product team would be experimenting with *how* to create these solutions and integrate them into new or existing products, as well as testing ideas and assumptions with the customer.

Helix replaces the feature roadmap that most companies use to build products and services. This reverses the inside-out approach, initiates the two-way conversation with the customer, and makes room for innovation. It provides enough structure to enable the product team to focus on their backlog of questions, assumptions, and risks along with creating and testing possible features, functionality, and user experiences. Imagine a product team composed of a product manager, a few designers, a couple of developers, someone from operations, and some other specialists who contribute from time to time. Helix enables—actually *encourages*—diverse teams like this, with widely varying experience and perspectives, to come together and collaboratively own a product and customer experience end-to-end.

HELIX RECAP

Helix is an iterative framework that produces innovation, alignment, and transformation in situations that change fast and have deeply interconnected moving parts. Helix solves for isolated, siloed products that don't address your customer's whole experience or solution. It provides the means for optimizing product value without missing the chance to revolutionize your market or industry.

Helix is a framework that encourages diversity and makes use of multiple points of view, giving everyone on the product team the means to work collaboratively. The iterative divergent/convergent nature of Helix is easily linked to agile sprints and team backlogs. The experimentation and reflection built into Helix reinforce lean-agile practices. And the Helix cycle can be leaderless, calling for and utilizing a framework for self-managed, self-governed, and self-organizing teams.

KEY TAKEAWAYS: HELIX

Executives:

Business and technical agility are now intertwined with, not separate from, organizational change. This means your strategy must integrate the two seamlessly to create and deliver customer value. At the corporate level IT can no longer be the department of automation and cost-cutting; it must start being the department of value creation, which allows you to merge offerings from multiple lines of business into new, exciting customer experiences, what we call *economies of synergy*.

Executive teams can use the same Helix process that the product development teams use to update business models, radically redesign siloed lines of business, and even perform mergers and acquisitions (the two vectors defining the activities of each company that produces their integration). The benefit of this is that Helix is designed to work across the organizational stack and functional boundaries, bringing people together to drive change.

Lastly, Helix helps executives stay out of the weeds. Focus your attention on how the two vectors affect each other. This defines your role in the product development process, is a contribution that only you can make, and allows for autonomous, self-managed teams.

Transformation Leaders:

To deliver customer value, new organizational structures and relationships are needed and old out-of-date processes and power centers (for example, finance and demand/change management) need a radical makeover. To do this you need to avoid the lift-and-shift approach to applying agile practices to business, which oversimplifies the digital transformation required in large corporations.

Transformational leaders need to focus on macro-level portfolio management rather than on micro-level portfolios, constantly integrating dynamic changes in the market ecosystem, technological advances, and user desires. The most critical, if most difficult, role you play is helping product development teams make the change from projects to products. There is no right way to do this, no set of defined roles and responsibilities. It is something that you design and develop based on your existing organizational structure and job descriptions.

Adopting a customer perspective also expands the definition of the product team; since products are larger and more relationally complex than projects, they incorporate multiple stakeholders from across organizational boundaries. In the process, roles and responsibilities need to change, with some being phased out while others are broadened. Your role is to provide feedback loops that enable dynamic rebalancing of the product teams' thinking and approaches without prolonging the product development lifecycle. Using the two Helix vectors allows you to imagine product concepts linked to future market scenarios and even to test them in the market.

Managers:
The challenge and opportunity for you is to build a culture of exploration, experimentation, and evidence-based decision-making. This requires new tools that enable collaboration and cooperation to drive innovation and transformation. Using the Helix framework, you can work with your teams to imagine the broader requirements and relationships their products need (upper vector) and to integrate these into the daily activities of development (lower vector).

Become a facilitator of the takeoff, midpoint, and landing sessions, working *on* the organization rather than *in* it. Learn to be a boundary spanner and information broker so that you can work across the networks that emerge from applying the Helix process tactically. Make part of your role in the Helix process ensuring that experiments are well designed and carried out.

As a leader, your role is developing others, rather than being a subject matter expert who happens to have direct reports. Helix can easily be applied to people, the upper vector to track their skills and knowledge and the lower for their daily activities. This brings your coaching to the objective-activity level, providing almost real-time feedback for behavioral change. Use the AIM and huddle format(s) to work with people to make their growth visible, cocreated, and achievable.

Employees:

Helix puts creativity back in your work and provides the path for learning and knowledge. Use the top vector to drive your imagination and challenge your thinking; use the lower vector to run your experiments and validate your ideas.

When you are part of a product development unit, you are part of an ecosystem of diverse colleagues. Helix is a framework that allows you to learn collectively and to practice the skills of self-management, self-governance, and self-organization. It has just enough structure to help you implement your ideas without running off the rails. Along with the Helix process, the tools within Helix (Figures 6.3-6.5) provide ways to develop your ideas, your skills, and your career. Use these to expand your role, knowledge, and relationships.

INTERMEZZO
Achieving Exceptional Performance

Anna sits at the pub bar, absently swirling a glass of wine. Abe is on his way to meet her for dinner and a chat about goal setting. Good timing, she thinks; she has just finished her fourth quarter OKRs (objectives and key results) and that's something that Abe could probably use. Anna's company had first started using OKRs when they were only a bit further along in the digital journey than Abe is right now. Since then, their technology has advanced dramatically, they are now moving into Wave 4 in many parts of the business, and the organization is composed of loosely coupled microbusiness units. As the company has grown, they've diversified, using the creativity and exploration power that OKRs provide to push themselves, their business, and even the entire entertainment industry.

"I'm finally here," Abe pants. "The traffic was so bad that I gave up on the cab and jogged the last part of the way."

"Impressive," Anna laughs. "Now you really deserve a drink and dinner. Shall we find a table?"

When they are settled and have caught up on work in general, Abe jumps right to the point, "Anna, the fourth quarter is starting, and I have to set goals for next year. It will take me all quarter to get everything ready to launch in January. I want to include the digital transformation in next year's goals, but it usually takes till March," Abe groans, "for teams and individuals to finally set *their* goals. There has to be a better way! I figured that you might have some ideas."

"You're right about needing a better way. How many goals do you usually cascade down?" Anna asks.

"I usually get five or so from corporate and add another five of my own, with the transformational goals . . . I'm afraid the list is going to be long," Abe says grimly.

Anna looks shocked for a moment, then goes on. "Ok, what's the overarching strategy for the company right now, the strategy that you are setting these goals to achieve?"

"Well, we are moving to digital. And switching from funding projects to funding products; it's a big deal and is creating disruption." Abe pauses, then furrows his brows. "Still, though these are important, they don't really constitute a strategy. And I know that every business needs to make money, but that isn't a strategy either. Unfortunately, that really does seem to be our focus, if you look at how we incentivize people. Lame, huh?"

"*Yeah*," Anna's face has gone from stunned to outright disbelief. "Your strategy has to give people a better reason than just compensation to come to work and contribute their all. It has to be *meaningful!*"

Anna goes on, "Listen, Abe: Are you willing to try something really different? Something that will unleash creativity and engagement?" Abe nods, so she continues, "Well, the first thing you need is a strategy that not only provides direction, but, more importantly, makes me, your employee, want to come to work and kick butt. *Based on that*, you write three to five goals that focus the whole organization on how, at a high level, we are going to achieve that strategy. Then you have everyone write quarterly OKRs, objectives and key results, that describe how *each* is going to contribute to your goals and strategy. Are you with me so far?"

It's Abe's turn to be shocked. "Quarterly? If we can't get yearly goals done until March, what is the point of quarterly?"

"That is exactly the point!" Anna continues. "You have a system that doesn't encourage agility, let alone the ability to take advantage of business opportunities and changes in the marketplace. Abe, *you* are taking on all the hard work of moving to digital and integrating your technology teams with the business. Do you really think you can steer that boat a year at a time? No, clearly not! And my guess is that you don't really know what the individuals across your organization are working on, how they are contributing to your strategy. Right?"

Abe nods.

"How much would you give for complete transparency?" Anna asks.

"How much do you want?" Abe replies. Anna laughs and shakes her head.

Over dinner, Anna walks Abe through Strive, a performance management system that her company uses that is based on OKRs. Abe scratches lots of notes and, while waiting for coffee and dessert, summarizes what he has learned.

"So, there is only one set of goals, right? The rest are objectives and key results. Objectives are written to be aspirational, so there aren't many of them; and they have quantitative key results written as a moonshot, which is what I *am* really trying to achieve, not just for show. If I achieve the 70 percent level, I have really moved the needle for the business and the customer." Abe pauses to consider that, "Still trying to get my head around that one! Anyway," he sighs, "a big part of success comes from horizontal links to other teams, and these can and should span functional and organizational boundaries. Finally, anyone, even I, can play a contributor role and participate in a team's OKRs." He folds his hands in front of himself with satisfaction. "So how am I doing so far?"

"So far so good," Anna replies. "Of course you skipped the goal network and the huddles — which are key to transparency."

Abe nods and adds these to his list.

"When all the OKRs are published to the goal network, everyone can see all the work being done for the quarter," Anna says. "*You* can see all the work being done. And you can make sure that funding and resources are being applied to the most important work. All your leaders can connect people to the work they can contribute to and learn from. Career development in action!"

"Didn't think about that." Abe scribbles more notes.

Anna pauses until he finishes. "Listen, Strive huddles are the cornerstone to transparency and can really drive your transformation. Remember those weekly ceremonies that the teams have?"

Abe frowns, struggling to remember.

"When they ask themselves the six questions?" Anna continues. "The answers to those six questions provide a treasure trove of data that you can turn into knowledge the whole organization can use. Imagine publishing a monthly list of the top ten breakthroughs. Or publicly rewarding the contributor who solved a gnarly impediment. How about having a learning site where folks can go to browse and pick up tips and ideas for their own work. And don't forget what it is like to be on a team that records the high points of the week for all its members. This is your culture shift, Abe. This is where people and behaviors change."

In the cab home Abe ponders this new way of working. Adopting Strive would be a transformation in itself. Still the dots seem to connect — this fits right into the Helix framework that Gina had taught him last month! That sends his mind racing forward, and he grabs his notebook yet again. Who knew, Abe muses to himself, that digital transformation could be so exciting? He hasn't been this enthusiastic and motivated about work in years.

Chapter 7

Strive Framework — Advance Breakthrough Performance

In late 1999 John Doerr spoke to the Google management team about a growth regimen for the fledgling company. His plan was built on OKRs (objectives and key results), a goal-setting process Doerr had learned at Intel. This scheme removed the ad hoc goals set by Sergey Brin and Larry Page while supporting a simple process that maintained the "think big" ethos of the founders, one that avoided the common tendency of managers' simply trying to look good by overdelivering.

Doerr's intent was to tighten decision-making, focus the company around a few key objectives, and rigorously measure progress against these objectives. OKRs were initiated first quarter 2000 with initial objectives such as "move toward market leadership," "(offer) best search user experience," "meet or exceed revenue plan," and "improve internal organization."[1] The company chose to maintain these objectives for many quarters, though the key results changed quarterly. KRs were aggressive, metric heavy, and action-oriented.

For example, head of sales Omid Kordestani's first quarter objective was to book $500,000 in ad revenue by the end of 1Q2000.[2] This was not only the first quarter of their advertising program, but was also well before AdWords (an online advertising service developed by Google, where advertisers pay to display brief advertising copy, product listings, and video content to web users[3]) had launched. For Google, with a sales group of just six people and anonymity outside of the Silicon Valley, this was a moonshot. Yahoo, their main competitor, was cutting deeply discounted deals with their advertisers, and Google's search platform was still a bit wonky, with engineering issues, flakey infrastructure, and incomplete tools. Page and Brin insisted that the KR for this objective count only money in the bank and committed sales, no "maybe"s or even strong leads.

At the end of the quarter, the whole company gathered to review the corporate results, and, by then, literally scores of the quarters OKRs. With much fanfare, Kordestani revealed his banked revenue for the quarter as $636,000, with more than $1 million in overall revenue commitments.

OKRs are an example of Google's culture of transparency

---

1 Douglas Edwards, *I'm Feeling Lucky: The Confessions of Google Employee Number 59,* Houghton Mifflin Harcourt, New York, NY, 2011.

2 Ibid.

3 Wikipedia, https://en.wikipedia.org/wiki/AdWords.

coupled with the ideal of setting almost unattainable goals.[4] Anyone in the company can find a person's OKRs; they are published in
the corporate phone directory, right next to their name and phone
number. This enables people to learn what other people do, their
priorities, what they are working on, as well as what they care about.
"If someone else's OKRs were contingent on me, I wanted to be fore-
warned," explains Douglas Edwards, "and I wanted to know that the
people whose help I would need to complete my own OKRs were
aware of them."[5] This meant that at the end of the quarter everyone
was in constant communication getting their OKRs completed.

To encourage risk-taking, another aspect of the Google culture, OKRs were removed from performance reviews and the
ideal achievement rate was set at 70 percent, not 100 percent. This
encouraged people to aim high and "believe in moonshots, which
cause you to achieve more in failure than you would in succeeding at a more modest goal."[6] As Googler Astro Teller, the lead on
Google Glass and the self-driving car, so eloquently put it: "If you
want your car to get 50 miles per gallon, fine. You can retool your
car a little bit. But if I tell you it has to run on a gallon of gas for
five hundred miles, you have to start over."[7] Still, wouldn't a 70 percent achievement—350 mpg—be awesome!? Of course this also
means that throughout the quarter status updates may be full of
yellow and red status buttons, but imagine how less impressive your

4 Eric Schmidt, Jonathan Rosenberg, *How Google Works*, Hachette Book Group,
   New York, NY, 2014.

5 Douglas Edwards, p. 54.

6 Laszlo Bock , *Work Rules: Insights from Inside Google That Will Transform How You Live
   and Lead,* Twelve, New York, NY, 2015, p. 334.

7 Ibid.

company would be if consistent green status updates simply indicated sandbagging!

As they grew the company, Page and Brin used OKRs to rapidly respond to change and opportunity in the market. Google expects "instantaneous" results, and products live or die based on speed and data, not sentiment. From the beginning, even the CEOs would write OKRs and host company-wide meetings to discuss them. During these sessions all product and business leaders talk through their OKRs and publicly grade themselves and their group on the last quarter's performance, candidly discussing the ambitious objectives they didn't achieve. Public scoring by leadership, again usually full of yellow and red marks, allows people to honestly judge their own performance safely and without being tracked. Market focused OKRs also mean that teams that are grossly out of alignment stand out and can be addressed.

With OKRs hammered out between the business and product leadership, people and/or teams are ready to create their own OKRs with little doubt of the company's focus for the quarter. Once you see the corporate goals and people's OKRs, it is easy to compare yours to them and either remain on course or readjust one's path.

At Google OKRs are not comprehensive. Business as Usual (BAU) work does not require OKRs, only those products and programs that need the extra focus, care, and feeding do. Google believes that this keeps people from chasing the competition, adopting a me-too or fast-follow-on strategy, and encourages innovation and growth.

Google, Spotify, LinkedIn, and Zynga are all examples of organizations conceived by their founders as digital native companies. Not surprisingly, all of them view central control and traditional management as a liability in digital markets, where product life cycles are a fraction of those launched before 2000. Each in its own way has pioneered new agile management practices that amplify autonomy and team decision-making, pushing responsibility to where it is most expedient and people are the most informed. Despite the diversity of management innovations across these digital companies, all of these firms adopted the OKR framework for mobilizing organizational alignment and breakthrough performance.

Pushing decision-making and accountability deep into the organization is essential and foundational to the operating model of digital natives. OKRs work because they create a common and unambiguous understanding of company goals and intended quarterly business outcomes, galvanizing the entire organization to focus on what matters most (see sidebar). OKRs are the antidote to waterfall planning, funding projects instead of products, and alignment practices built for the industrial age. For those of you using agile software execution methods, such as Scrum, think of OKRs as agile corporate goal setting *for the entire company.*

So we're saying that OKRs work and should be used; but how?

The OKRs that digital native companies use are deceptively simple to describe (though, for various reasons we'll unpack later in this chapter, they lack the operational robustness critical to disrupting larger traditional companies seeking to reinvent themselves for digital). The fundamentals of OKRs, which we call OKRs 1.0, are perhaps more important to understand at this point because they serve as the foundation of a new OKRs 2.0 system we've developed called *Strive.* Strive is a next-generation OKR system focused on performance management for traditional companies moving to the digital age, one that dramatically improves their ability to navigate their digital transformation.

OKRs 1.0 helps organizations align and perform by asking teams to define a few powerful objectives and their associated key results in order to achieve corporate strategy and goals. Objectives are intended to be moonshots, outcomes that would truly move the performance and value creation needle. Key results are quantitative and force teams to question, even rethink, how they approach the challenges and opportunities of the objective. In this chapter, we move on to highlight the breakthrough benefits of the Strive OKR 2.0 system and show you how they amplify the *Helix*

First-generation OKRs start by asking senior leaders to answer four questions:

First, what is the mission of your business? Express it as a clear, enduring, even inspiring purpose. We are not talking about superficial marketing speak. Also, the answer is not to make money. That is the byproduct of fulfilling your company's mission.

Second, what is your company's core strategy for achieving your mission? Explaining this gets tricky because larger firms often have difficulty fashioning and articulating a strategy that applies to all of their diverse business units and that every employee in the company can understand. But that's exactly the point. Agility at scale is about empowering every employee and team to step into authentic partnership and take daily responsibility for making decisions that advance the company's strategy.

Third, what are your company's two or three goals for the next four quarters that are essential to achieving the company's longer-term strategy? Just two or three goals, really? You bet. If expressed at the right level of ambition, two to three goals are the right focus for an entire company.

Fourth—and often the most challenging—what are the two to three most critical objectives for your company to pursue in the next quarter that are likely to lead to overachievement of the annual goals? In other words, how would you prioritize the goals you've created?

framework for those seeking a more detailed practitioner guide on how to implement this new performance management system in your company.

For now let's dive into how we've reinvented first generation OKRs to help traditional firms accelerate more quickly through each of the digital waves. What we've learned over the last 20 years of agile software development is that attaining longer-term outcomes (like delivering a large digital platform) is more likely when you break the work down into smaller, more meaningful increments. OKR 1.0 does this. Now we need the means to transform large enterprises into communities of autonomous teams, directionally focused at the global level (strategy) and wildly creative and ambitious at the local level. Strive OKR 2.0 achieves this.

BOTTOMS UP:
CASCADING OBJECTIVES FROM BELOW

Imagine CEOs of traditional companies routinely celebrating a mere 70 percent level of achievement of a team's contribution to strategic corporate goals. It isn't going to happen. But first-generation OKRs encourage companies to define objectives and key results to be so aspirational that achieving 70 percent *is* commended, and this works quite well in digital native companies where OKRs are so ambitiously constructed that failure isn't seen as failure, but instead as *progress.*

However, in traditional companies, risk-taking and failure are still largely discouraged by culture, politics, and incentives. For this reason, we saw the need for a completely new way to effect risk-taking and overachievement; we wanted to encourage cultural change by rewarding ambitious achievement and making risk-taking and failure safe. This has been achieved with the novel Strive OKR scoring system.

To make OKRs 2.0 more comprehensive, we created a scoring system that provides teams with three levels of accomplishment (see sidebar). For each KR, teams are asked to write outcomes that describe degrees of difficulty: 0.3 is either BAU or a necessary, but not sufficient, foundation for innovation; 0.7 moves the needle for the business or customer; and 1.0 is a moonshot. This enables teams to imagine three different paths to success, and generate three work plans for their quarter. It also gives BAU teams the means to participate: 0.3 would be minimal, maintenance work; 0.7 work that delivers the highest BAU value to the business; 1.0 an innovative way they might contribute or collaborate with others. Most importantly, this happens *at the beginning* of the quarter (rather than at the end in retrospection) and causes teams to consider collaborative partners they will need to truly make an impact.

OKRs break with traditional goal alignment by challenging teams across the organization to thoughtfully consider the company's goals and to align their daily work to them. In this way, teams can *independently* decide what specific objectives and key results they'll work on to provide the company the best opportunity for achieving corporate goals, even leading to market game-changers if fully achieved. This cannot be overemphasized. It places employee creativity as central to strategy.

If you're like most, you may be skeptical about how this approach could possibly work across thousands of teams in a global organization without encouraging either sandbagging or chaos. The answer is simple: All team commitments activate two powerful forces that drive team performance and company outcomes. First, all teams and their commitments are public to the entire company. This level of transparency triggers the positive aspects of social pressure (fitting in) and reciprocity (assisting others), discouraging teams from writing OKRs that are either poorly aligned with company goals or simply not challenging enough. Second, transparency *plus* autonomy activate a powerful new company-wide conversation

Strive Key Result Score 0.3 —
Expected, Competent Outcomes

Reaching this KR score is typically within the team's control.
For this reason, it requires no explicit commitments
from outside subject matter experts or adjacent teams.
The progress the team makes is challenging but not
groundbreaking for the firm.

Strive Key Result Score 0.7 —
Moving the Needle for the Corporation

Those familiar with first-gen OKRs will notice that we didn't
include a halfway achievement point (0.5). Why? After many
field experiments and reviews with other OKR practitioners, it
became clear that targeting 0.5 KRs did very little to influence
overall company performance.

However, it turns out that it's rare for teams to achieve a 1.0
KR score without also crossing a critical threshold. Hence,
if a 1.0 OKR is considered a moonshot, then think of 0.7
as the critical threshold and a major triumph. Achieving
0.7 represents breakthroughs in thinking and producing

that serves to further clarify, invigorate, and galvanize the company.
Team members can participate in delivering outcomes that matter
not just to them, but to the entire organization.

Further exploiting the power of social reciprocity, we've intentionally designed our OKRs 2.0 system with an interesting twist. Unlike
with OKRs 1.0, no team in your company can be considered an active
member of the quarterly OKR process unless and until it can secure
negotiated and personal commitments from others in support of its
1.0 moonshot. That's right. If a team joins the company's quarterly
journey toward hyperalignment and achievement, its 1.0 KRs must

significant company overachievement, just not as insanely ambitious as a moonshot. In defining 0.7 KRs, teams are also required to acknowledge and negotiate key horizontal dependencies with other teams, dependencies that are essential to a successful end result.

Strive Key Result Score 1.0 —
Your Moonshot

Similar to first-gen KRs, Strive KR scores of 1.0 represent a real moonshot outcome. Such outcomes have the potential, if achieved, to be game-changing for your entire firm. But unlike in digital native companies, doing something truly game-changing for a large traditional company could rarely happen within a single team. Instead, company-wide breakthroughs in traditional firms require broad horizontal collaboration, alignment, and joint contribution and sacrifice. Notice we didn't say vertical alignment. It turns out that vertical alignment in traditional firms is relatively easy when compared with the more complex and politically thorny challenge of getting those in adjacent silos to prioritize working together over the priorities of their respective divisions or functional silos.

have a minimum of two commitments from other teams in order to contribute to outcomes necessary for their moonshot KR.

Requiring these horizontal commitments makes KR scores of 0.7 and 1.0 more likely to produce results; it's what makes Strive OKRs so special. Giving teams the responsibility to negotiate explicit cross-organizational commitments generates collaborative breakthrough performance and operational cooperation, not to mention a way to transfer learning and innovative ideas.

A second change we've made is to who writes OKRs. First-gen OKRs push the expectation of OKR commitments down to the level of a single employee. The idea is that if vertical alignment is good, then taking it down to the level of individual employee behavior makes sense. But we have pivoted away from this idea to offer a different way forward:

We know from our decades of corporate experience that teams, not individual employees, are the foundation of work and innovation. While we maintain the individual commitment and behavioral change within the structure of team OKRs 2.0 by requiring individual employees to take responsibility for a given key result, this is a voluntary role on the *team* that encourages employee engagement and participation. But it is the teams—especially when they're autonomous and self-managing—that provide the means to clearly and concisely plan their work . . . and to share it with others through cooperation and collaboration. With this, alignment (vertical and horizontal) becomes possible.

Innovation is another critical reason we make OKRs a team-level activity. OKRs bring a strategic focus to every team in your company. Although an individual can be an internal entrepreneur (as in the case of 3M's Post-it Notes, Google's Gmail, and Gore's Glide Floss), an individual cannot produce a product singlehandedly. Armed with OKRs 2.0, these internal entrepreneurs can assemble an OKR team and, in full transparency, align their ideas with the highest-level corporate goals and with other team OKRs, both horizontally and vertically.

BOTTOM LINE:
ALIGNING PRODUCT BACKLOGS WITH COMPANY GOALS

One of the first changes we've made to OKRs reflects the extraordinary importance of language, which we covered in Chapter 5. Read any goal-setting book, or investigate any OKR tool, and you'll soon encounter what we call the babble of terms and definitions. For this reason, our first design challenge was to address the word *goal*.

In most companies, and in first-gen OKRs, the word *goal* crops up everywhere and seems to refer to almost anything. In OKRs 2.0, however, the word *goal* is used to communicate *only* the most strategic corporate-level outcomes sought by executive leadership. These corporate-level goals provide the scaffolding for teams across the rest of the organization to directionally align their OKRs. By limiting the use of the word *goal*, we make it clear to everyone in the company that there is *only one set of corporate goals*. From this foundation all teams are free to craft OKRs that are specific to their position in the company without drifting from or diluting the corporate strategy.

This challenges executive leaders to write goals that are meaningful, aspirational, and, especially, understandable. As teams translate the company's strategy and goals into explicit OKRs, it is essential that they are encouraged to check with executives above them, those leaders responsible for defining the direction that the entire company is taking. Ask them, "Could you clarify the company goals? If we deliver these OKRs, are we heading in the strategic direction you intend?"

Our design conversations also revealed a new and powerful OKRs 2.0 insight, one that executives can use to evaluate the clarity of their strategy. As groups write and post their OKRs, particularly after a large part of the company is participating in OKRs 2.0, executives can perform gap analyses between their *espoused strategy* (what the executives intend) and the actual *strategy in use* — derived from the actual OKRs. In other words, as OKRs are written and published, we can probe the language and outcomes they contain. Executive teams can ask themselves: How does our intended strategy manifest itself in the written OKRs? Are we going to accomplish what we need to? And, are we funding the efforts that really make a difference?

For executives trying to innovate and transform their organization, how their strategy is manifested is essential. Currently, you likely have no reliable way to reveal the company's strategy in use, the one that the company is collectively pursuing under your radar, and you may be falling back on considering—through budget requests and vendor statements of work—only financial outcomes.

Before OKR 2.0, executives communicated the espoused strategy and hoped that people interpreted it the way they intended it. But now you can actually analyze your how your strategy is coming through based on performance: Are different parts of the business attacking a goal in disconnected or counterproductive ways? Do people understand what we are trying to improve and why? Or, from the customer's point of view: Which OKRs are having the biggest impact on customer satisfaction? Is the effort seamlessly coordinated across all the customer touch points? And: What does improved customer experience (your intended strategy) mean to the various parts of the company? Are resources sufficiently focused to move the customer experience needle?

When you can visualize your strategy in action, you get a view of other workings of the company, things such as pockets of rebellion, mavericks that may or may not be advancing your intention, or positive deviants and how they are influencing different parts of the company, producing innovative ideas that spread from one part of the company to another. Now we have transparency at the strategic level, not just the activity level. This is how and why corporate executives can amplify and/or dampen the execution of their strategy throughout the year without inducing the whiplash of pivots and course changes.

A second way that leaders, managers, and team members can track strategic alignment is by examining team backlogs. First-gen OKRs make no attempt to explicitly connect OKR commitments to things like agile product backlogs or individual/team performance. But they should, and they can. As product innovation and organizational transformation practitioners, we've spent nearly two decades working with digital and product engineering teams, and we've notice that somewhere along the way agile practices have become untethered from higher-level corporate strategy and, unfortunately, they now lack accountability for alignment with strategic goals. This is one of the main reasons business leaders tell us they are reluctant to adopt agile on their side of the house.

Would it surprise you if we told you that, on average, 60 percent or more of agile product team backlogs are not well aligned with company strategy and goals? Probably not; in fact, the results of our own client backlog reviews in the last few years has averaged closer to 65 percent. But why? On the surface, this misalignment seems impossible. Aren't agile product backlogs supposed to be prioritized by business product owners (PO) in ways that maximize value creation?

Keep in mind that in larger traditional companies there are literally hundreds of products and product backlogs, each being optimized for value creation and primarily concerned with the customers and users of that particular product or service. This is the systems problem of optimizing the parts and not the whole. In digital native companies, often one single, large product is the focus of the corporate strategy and all work being done to achieve it. It is this difference that causes traditional corporate product backlogs to become misaligned with company priorities and goals. However, as digital natives grow they are not immune to this phenomenon.

Our next-gen OKR system addresses this directly by linking OKR commitments to local product backlogs. This encourages transparent decisions about backlog prioritization and delivering features aligned to corporate strategy. To be clear, we are not suggesting that every product backlog in a larger company be 100 percent aligned with OKRs — that would squelch innovation. But it's also clear that having product backlogs that average just 35–40 percent alignment with your company's priorities is a surefire strategy for corporate and product mediocrity — or worse.

To overcome backlog misalignment and to reduce dependencies we created two new roles for OKR 2.0 teams: KR Champion and Horizontal Partner.

Achieving awesome and succeeding at moonshots can rarely be done by a single team, perhaps not even a single line of business. Product innovation that disrupts the market and delights customers requires a holistic view of corporate assets as they apply to customer needs, bridging business silos, and simplifying customer interactions. OKR 2.0 achieves this by formalizing a way for teams to reach across organizational and functional boundaries to collaborate and coordinate their work.

Members of teams who take on the responsibility to directly advance KRs are called *KR Champions*. They usually volunteer, telling their team members: "Hey, I want to be the champion for this KR."

The KR champion polishes the KR, ensuring that it is crafted to challenge the thinking of the team and to identify other teams complementary or foundational to their OKR and on whom they are relying.

Part of the job also entails the KR champion's recruiting people, going beyond the abstract "We need marketing or technology to provide x." These recruits, *horizontal partners,* have the influence and willingness to manage a horizontal dependency, one that falls outside the requesting team's immediate purview. Linking up with others is personal for the KR champion. It involves one-on-one relationships, and is a catalyst for authentic cross-boundary collaboration and cooperation.

Finally, horizontal partners play dual roles: the role of collaborative third-opinion subject matter expert for the KR team, *and* the role of coordinator, recruiting the teams that they lead, teams who the KR champion relies on to achieve their amazing outcome. By agreeing to become part of the KR's success, the horizontal partner is removed from becoming a potential impediment or accidental adversary. Instead, these individuals become core collaborators and enablers of the team's success.

THE ELEPHANT IN THE ROOM:
OLD-SCHOOL TALENT MANAGEMENT

We all know that company employees are traditionally organized into one of three categories: executives, managers, and *everyone else . . .* with the *everyone else* category representing the vast majority. It only follows that, if real transformation is going to happen, it will be the result of tapping into this massive group.

In companies today most of these *everybody else* employees are disengaged; and employee engagement scores have been stagnant for years. When you aggregate several of the more recent and well-regarded employee engagement studies, you find a staggering 56 percent of employees are not engaged, and only 28 percent are highly engaged.[8]

These engagement studies reveal several systemic organizational challenges. To overcome the obstacle of disengagement, we asked: How do we build an operational management system on top of OKRs to drive meaningful engagement that wins the hearts and minds of everyone in the company?

Although first-generation OKRs encourage deep engagement

---

8 Amy Adkins, "Employee Engagement in U.S. Stagnant in 2015," Gallup, January 13, 2016, http://www.gallup.com/poll/188144/employee-engagement-stagnant-2015.aspx; Aon, *2015 Trends in Global Employee Engagement: Making Engagement Happen* (London: Aon, 2015), http://www.aon.com/attachments/human-capital-consulting/2015-Trends-in-Global-Employee-Engagement-Report.pdf; Harvard Business Review Analytic Services, *The Impact of Employee Engagement on Performance* (Boston: Harvard Business School Press, 2013), https://hbr.org/resources/pdfs/comm/achievers/hbr_achievers_report_sep13.pdf.

and ownership of corporate goals at the individual-employee level, they also introduce confusion and conflict with talent management practices because they *intentionally exclude* employee OKR achievement from employee merit and promotion reviews. Additionally, traditional performance reviews and merit raise practices remain relics from the past. We think keeping OKRs and employee talent management separate is a huge missed opportunity. By keeping OKRs at the team level, we eliminate confusion between employee performance and OKR achievement *and* enable the inclusion of OKR contribution as part of individual performance.

We further know that diverse groups of problem solvers consistently outperform individuals *as well as* groups composed of the best and the brightest.[9] For these reasons we've operationalized the practice of OKR achievement into what we call a Strive Huddle (see sidebar and Figure 6.5 for graphic).

Huddles are exactly what they appear they would be: lightweight "coming together" occasions that encourage teams to make use of their individual diversity. Huddles help team members learn collectively. Furthermore, they drive teams to overcome obstacles and predict forward progress rather than simply tracking historical progress. Structured to make contribution easy for members and nonmembers alike, huddles take advantage of social physics and group dynamics, providing the most accurate

---

9 Peter Gloor and Scott Cooper, *Coolhunting: Chasing Down the Next Big Thing* (New York: AMACOM, 2007); Jeff Howe, *Crowdsourcing: Why the Power of the Crowd Is Driving the Future of Business* (New York: Crown Business, 2009); Scott E. Page, *The Difference: How the Power of Diversity Creates Better Groups, Firms, Schools, and Societies* (Princeton, NJ: Princeton University Press, 2008); Philip E. Tetlock and Dan Gardner, *Superforecasting: The Art and Science of Prediction* (New York: Broadway Books, 2016).

During the weekly Team Huddle each team member answers the following questions, allowing the team to judge their progress toward KR 1.0:

• What new impediments have I encountered?

• What breakthroughs have I made in my work?

• What key learning do I want to bring to the attention of the team?

• What was my personal high point this week, and why?

• What next steps can I take to make progress on this KR, and what outcome do I expect this to produce?

• What insights have we uncovered during this huddle that should be shared with other Strive teams in the organization?

The team tracks the accuracy of their forecast each week and improves their prediction skills by reviewing the following questions:

• Looking back, what impacted our confidence last week?

• Were there weak signals (a mishap or unexpected event) that we ignored, discounted, or placed too much emphasis on?

• Are we focusing on breakthroughs or impediments to the detriment of learning and progress?

• Do we have the right people in the conversation?

• How are we using the forecasting trends to inform our work going forward?

• Are we asking the right questions?

• Are we getting better at forecasting, and, if not, what can we do to improve?

indications of how the team is doing over the entire OKR period.[10]

We recommend that huddles be held either at the end of each week or the beginning of each week. During the week, team members and contributors (employees who opt in to contribute to a KR in a specific way but are not team members) capture their progress by answering the huddle questions about the KR on which they are working. These answers promote rapid learning and innovation.

The KR champion collects all of the insights and synthesizes them. During the huddle, they are explored with the extended team (anyone who chooses to join) to gain insights, correct course, jump ahead, and recognize the work of the team. Similar to what occurs in a prediction market, at the end of the collective conversation a crowd-sourced forecast for each KR is made: Are we on track to hit our 0.7 or 1.0 target? How confident can we be in this prediction? This forecast is composed of the diverse knowledge and experience of all team members and contributors.

Strive huddles can and should be active learning experiences rather than status updates. They turn OKRs into a powerful operational framework that accelerates learning, innovation, and organizational agility. Team members contribute transparently because it is safe to do so. Executives and leaders above, below, and around each team can see the work it is doing weekly and provide encouragement and support. Ultimately, data mining the output

---

10 Teresa Amabile and Steven Kramer, *The Progress Principle: Using Small Wins to Ignite Joy, Engagement, and Creativity at Work* (Boston: Harvard Business Review Press, 2011); Kim S. Cameron and Robert E. Quinn, *Diagnosing and Changing Organizational Culture: Based on the Competing Values Framework*, 3rd ed., (San Francisco: Jossey-Bass, 2011); Alex Pentland, *Social Physics: How Social Networks Can Make Us Smarter*, reissue ed. (New York: Penguin Books, 2015); Richard H. Thaler and Cass R. Sunstein, *Nudge: Improving Decisions About Health, Wealth, and Happiness*, rev. ed. (New York: Penguin Books, 2009).

of huddles across the company can be a way to search for fresh, innovative ideas, not to mention a way to connect the knowledge dots across an enterprise that is huge, global, and serving many different markets.

Along with the critical role of teams, enterprise HR executives know that innovation and organizational agility are tied to attracting and motivating the best talent. And although a significant number of Fortune 500 companies have eliminated their performance management process in its current form, talent management over the last decade remains hit or miss. For this reason, our next-gen OKR system is also designed to specifically encourage employee engagement and contributions, particularly those that drive company performance and influence professional advancement.

The challenge of talent management is rooted in the organization. Social systems, including culture and tribal mindsets, seem to perpetuate an unfair, opaque set of practices that result in promotions, advancements, and pay increases that often have little to do with actual contribution to corporate strategy. Worse, rewards are more often than not linked to employee compliance. In the words of Todd Warner, founder of Like Minds Advisory, "Too often, CEOs say they're looking to promote talent but end up promoting familiarity . . . *They reward compliance, not creativity.*"[11] Ironically, these same executives extol the virtues of cultivating a culture of entrepreneurship and risk-taking, which is the very opposite of compliance!

This chasm, between the desire for employee engagement,

---

11 "3 Reasons Why Talent Management Isn't Working Anymore," *Harvard Business Review*, July 5, 2016, https://hbr.org/2016/07/3-reasons-why-talent-management-isnt-working-anymore?webSyncID=39d4cbe4-3443-8a8b-4543-eb7335518da2&sessionGUID=971bd1ee-cdcd-450e-e87d-492e856c199d.

risk-taking, and entrepreneurship and the reality that the daily grind of work renders employees invisible, is the real challenge. But the Strive performance management system provides a pragmatic, operationally grounded way for employees to enlist themselves, helping to advance the performance and strategic outcomes of the company itself—which is intrinsically rewarding in and of itself. Incidentally, it also provides ways to formally and officially reward them at the same time, as shall be seen.

A recent *Harvard Business Review* article about employee motivation puts this best: "Interactions with the beneficiaries of one's work [customers and senior executives] can be highly motivating because they heighten workers' perceptions of the impact of their work . . . In our studies, positive words from internal beneficiaries of employees' work—their colleagues—served as an important source of motivation by strengthening the workers' sense of belongingness."[12] So rather than ignoring OKR contributions in employee reviews, recognizing contributions made by individuals and teams allows employees to feel the direct impact they are having on the company's most crucial goals and outcomes.

In reinventing OKRs we looked for a way to harness the untapped creativity of all employees. To achieve this we've created the opportunity for any employee to work with an OKR team. We invite him or her to play a new role we call "contributor." Think of contributors as free agents, people who are not part of an OKR team but choose to work on a specific aspect related to a KR. The role requires zero approval from others, including an

---

12 Francesca Gino, "To Motivate Employees, Show Them How They're Helping Customers," *Harvard Business Review*, March 6, 2017, https://hbr.org/2017/03/to-motivate-employees-show-them-how-theyre-helping-customers?webSyncID=39d4cbe4-3443-8a8b-4543-eb7335518da2&sessionGUID=cbb66258-02d7-23a5-edd3-cac65c9ac276.

employee's manager. Thus, stepping into the role of contributor is open to literally anyone — individual, team member, manager, or even the CEO.

Inviting employees to step into the contributor role is simple. As Strive teams shape and finalize OKRs for the quarter, they publish these to all levels of the organization, creating what's called the Goal Network. By making team OKR commitments visible to all, we provide the operational means for employees who are not on a team to become contributors, to scan the network of OKRs and choose where and how to directly contribute.

Here's the cool part: These contributions don't have to be huge, perhaps a single phone call. In fact, contributors can often find opportunities to make multiple contributions across many OKRs throughout the organization during the quarter. This delivers what we know employees want most: autonomy, mastery, and purpose. Suddenly, we have a self-regulating system (regulated by corporate goals and strategy) that intrinsically rewards teams and individual contributors and benefits the entire company (not just a local department or team).

So far so good, you say, but what if these contributions aren't valuable? Or even worse, what if they distract employees from their day job? These are reasonable concerns that need to be explored.

Throughout the quarter Strive teams not only report their learning and achievements related to KRs during their huddle, but they also publish the impact that contributors' work had on their KRs. Think about that for a minute. Here is a way to invite any employee into active participation, encouraging your entire workforce to advance the outcomes that matter most to your company and to them, and then publicly reward them for their effort.

Not only are we exploiting the power of crowdsourcing, but the upside to employees is that the system isn't rigged. Contributors know that if their contributions have a positive impact on KR achievement, then both teams and the broader employee network will recognize them. This second-generation OKR innovation creates a powerful new way to recognize talent, reward success, and motivate employees.

And "talent management" takes on a new, easier, almost self-managing style that is less intimidating, more progressive — and more successful.

STRIVE RECAP

First-gen OKRs were not designed to disrupt traditional firms, only to optimize what were, mostly, digital natives. Strive, a next-generation OKRs system, is designed to *align* the enterprise, vertically and horizontally, *and* disrupt it. This align-disrupt process is critical to accelerating and successfully completing your company's digital wave journey.

Strive goal-setting becomes a clarifying process that starts when executives ask the question: What three to five goals would both deliver our strategy and maximize the potential for creativity and innovation across the organization? This *both/and* constraint provides what we are looking for: just enough structure to support work at the edge of chaos while encouraging organizational creativity.

Within this context, people writing OKRs can aim high and avoid business as usual. Strive teams create a diverse, highly adaptive structure outside of the org chart. Think of Strive teams as the means of bringing together a horizontal community of diverse problem solvers, all focused on innovative ways to tackle big challenges and opportunities.

This new structure and language for orchestrating OKRs across layers of the company broadens the *intent* of OKRs 2.0, moving them from a means of monitoring or tracking activities (like key performance indicators or management by objectives) to the tool we utilize to *enable organizational structure to emerge from the strategy we set.* In this way transparency is not solely focused on *what* teams and people are doing, it is also a window into *how* the organization is evolving — creating self-management, self-governance, and self-organization. This is how you transform fast.

While making the digital journey, Strive OKRs become the means for transforming to Wave 3 and beyond. Along with explicitly fostering diversity and increasing autonomy, OKRs linked to the Helix framework enable companies to transform from a Wave 1 hierarchical organization into a dynamic, heterogeneous ecosystem (Wave 3). Using the Helix framework to shift from projects to products, begins the digital transformation by simultaneously working *on and in* the organization; and when OKRs are a tool used to work *on and in* the organization, you are better able to see and exploit the rapid technology investments that you're making . . . to charge through the digital waves. By intentionally choosing a slice of the organization, say a line of business and its technical colleagues (CIO, CTO, teams . . . however you organize your company), you can combine Helix and Strive to provide the structure and planning for the transformation to digital one quarter at a time. Together, Helix and Strive provide a way to synergistically and rapidly integrate business and technology.

Finally, OKRs are a great way to understand what your business partners are trying to do. Read and understand their OKRs before writing your team's; look for other vertical links that support your work and let their OKRs broaden your OKRs. Attend the huddles of these teams when you can to listen to the conversation; reflect on their challenges and impediments, how do they impact your work and what could you do about it?

KEY TAKEAWAYS: STRIVE

Executives:

The act of putting quarterly planning in the hands of teams at all levels, while emphasizing delivering results that are game-changing for the company, is not just business as usual, it is core to why OKRs work so well. The fastest way to implement OKRs 2.0 is by using a top-down onboarding process, which paradoxically does not produce prescriptive cascading of goals.

If your company is moving from Wave 0 to Wave 1 (or from Wave 1 to Wave 2), we recommend that you create three levels of Strive OKR teams: summit (executive level), bridge (middle management), and field (the frontline doers; for example, agile software teams). This helps change organizational mindsets and culture by providing just enough structure.

There are very few ways to test your strategy in action; use Strive to see where and how it is playing out across the whole enterprise. This provides executives with endless opportunities to take advantage of *economies of synthesis,* which is a real bonus when integrating the physical with digital.

Transformation Leaders:

Digital generates a constant cycle of experimentation, learning, and change. By expanding the digital conversation from C-Suite to teams, OKRs focus talented people on a vision and a purpose, allowing them to achieve outstanding performance. Your task is to find the positive deviants in the mix and support them with resources, visibility, and information.

OKRs naturally inspire everyone to invest more deeply in their work — which drives achievement and accountability. Your job is to distribute the weight of strategy and goal achievement across the organization instead of on the shoulders of a few. Be a connector and boundary spanner based on the Goal Network.

Helix and Strive provide an integrated means for operationalizing your transformation strategy. Use them to make your aspirational future become concrete for those doing the work. Let their 2.0 KRs drive your imagination and set the pace of transformation across the enterprise.

Managers:

Make experimentation and failure safe by helping teams structure them into their OKRs. Use the 0.7 and 1.0 KRs to teach design thinking and to drive innovation.

Use the process of linking up with horizontal partners to transfer learning and ideas, potentially even bringing expertise into the team for a sprint or two. Make this the way you challenge thinking as well as established mindsets and behaviors. Encourage horizontal relationships that reduce dependencies between teams, but don't be afraid to connect to those far outside your domain of knowledge to bring in fresh ideas and perspectives.

You now have a new way to develop people and help them find a place in the Goal Network where they can be contributors. Coach teams to reach out across the organization to find new ideas, attract contributors, and huddle regularly. Use the huddle documentation to develop, recognize, and publicly reward people, both those who report to you and external contributors.

Employees:

It's time to stop simply working for the same company and to start working for the same outcome. Make the shift to ownership and growth when OKRs come your way; participate, don't just sit on the sidelines and watch. Be bold. Start thinking about cars that get 500 miles per gallon, not 50.

Whether or not you have OKRs in your company, when someone else's work is contingent on yours, work with them, become
horizontal partners. Become a connector, information broker, and
boundary spanner by acting on things others are doing that interest
you. Don't wait for permission to begin to develop your own personal goal network.

Abe's digital transformation faces a significant technical challenge: to lower the outage rate of 10 critical back office applications by 40 percent. Outages have been regularly taking their toll across the multiple corporate businesses that use these applications. Technical debt is too high, but so is social debt. As far as the businesses are concerned, technology has failed to increase the speed of issue resolution and uptime.

Sam's division of the company owns the problem and is working on the solution. Four months ago they were provided a budget of $40 million and given one year to transform 10 apps in the back office. They were granted complete control of execution (including program management oversight and governance), but they are struggling; technical and adaptive challenges keep surfacing, and the timeline is slipping. If they are going to achieve their aggressive goals in the time allotted, something has to change.

In spite of their current state, Abe feels optimistic. He now has a sense of how to intervene, and in what he knows to be a much better way than he would have three months ago. He has the language of transformation, a framework for how, and the means to focus the division on the outcomes they have to achieve. He is curious to see how his newly acquired knowledge can positively impact this challenge.

From this new perspective Abe notices that the management team providing oversight to the program seems heavy-handed, anxious about the time slipping away. Governance of the program has grown increasingly contentious and time-consuming. Abe can see that the problems they face are adaptive first, technical second—nobody is working *on* the problem, they are all drowning *in* it.

Abe wants to do something to make it easier for the division to save itself, yet not intervene directly. Sam, the VP of the division, needs to get the work done and feel good about how he does it. This is the perfect time to transform one of Abe's leaders and his division. He decides to drop by to see Sam, something he has done very rarely. 'Time for me to change my behavior,' he thinks, 'and not just focus on what others should do.'

"Hi Sam." Abe leans against the doorframe. "How's it going?"

Sam's eyes widen as he looks up from his computer screen. "If you mean 'How is the Rapid program going?'" Sam says sourly, "well, it isn't living up to the name I optimistically gave it! Our middle managers are not skilled leaders, Abe, and I may have to take over the program management myself."

"Wow," Abe says, settling himself across from Sam. "I had heard it was a slow start, but that sounds like a grim diagnosis."

"'Grim' is the word for it," says Sam.

"You sure the leadership of the middle managers is the problem?"

"Seems that way to me," Sam says, leaning back in his chair.

"I ask only because I've been learning a lot about transformation over the last couple of months, and it may not be your managers."

"No?" Sam tenses slightly.

"You may have a systemic problem," Abe says.

Sam relaxes. Clearly Abe's not here to criticize or apply pressure. Sam had heard that Abe was making some serious changes to the way the executive team was working toward their agile transformation; it seems that what he'd heard was more than just rumor.

Abe takes the look on Sam's face as a cue to continue. "You know, your organization is a system, just like the technical systems we build. Except it's a *human* system. You've got to realize, though, that it has it has similar dependencies. And dependencies in human systems are social — relational dependencies and social debt, for example. The human system requires maintenance and upgrades in the form of cultural change and leadership development. Is this something you'd be interested in learning about and applying to the Rapid program? I think it could really help. I've got some ideas about where to start, and I'd be happy to coach you through it."

Sam's eyes get even bigger. Yep, this is definitely a new Abe. Sam rubs his hands together, clears his throat, and takes the bait. "Sure, why not? What do you have in mind?"

Over the next hour Abe tells Sam about his personal transformational journey and what he's learned from Anna, Gina, and Ethan. As Sam engages, the two explore how to apply these techniques to the Rapid program. Finally, they settle on a plan that involves all of Sam's middle managers, not just those responsible for delivering Rapid. As part of the plan, Sam will travel to every site, sit down with small groups of six to eight managers, and, for a couple of hours, have a conversation . . . but Sam won't be the one doing the talking. He'll be asking questions and listening. Together Abe and Sam draft the questions.

Sam follows through in short order. When he returns from his travels, Sam tells Abe that all of his managers impressed him. "They get it," Sam says. "They know what's going on. And they have solutions to the problems that Rapid — and other programs — face."

Sam asks Abe to support him while he transforms his organization and the program. Abe smiles.

"I want to go on a journey through Helix, Abe. I'm not sure what that means or how the heck to do it, but we need to continue to turn around the Rapid program. I can see that we need to develop real leadership in all of my managers, including my senior leadership team."

Sam sits back and waits for Abe to respond.

Abe nods, seeing a reflection of himself; this isn't the same person he had sent off on this mission. Somewhere along the way curiosity had built confidence and replaced desperation. Sam trusts himself and his managers much more than he had before.

"You got it," Abe says. "And I have an idea. My leadership team just experienced an adaptive leadership program to help us create a transformational backlog for the move to digital. Does that sound like a first step you might want to take, an experiment that might yield some interesting results?"

Sam's transformation begins with 120 managers participating in a two-day leadership experience delivered by an external consultant. By including all of his managers, Sam ensures that when the Rapid managers, in particular, change their behaviors, their peers across the organization will understand and be supportive. It provides a social platform: Everyone has the same language, an introduction to Helix (organizational change) and Strive (OKRs), and a chance to be in conversation about the very real technical and adaptive challenges they face. Adaptive leadership also introduces the concept of middle manager networks, a new role for management that increases their ability to create value.

Abe sits in on one session and is impressed with what he sees. These are people who care, who understand, and who are committed to delivering results. After the session Sam jumps into solution mode. "Abe, I really like that middle network idea. I'm thinking it would help the Rapid program. Would you support that? It might be risky, and I would have to reorganize the way we are approaching the program, but at this point I think it would be very helpful."

On the spot Abe decides to *follow yes*. Together, they devise their second experiment.

Top-down control would be gone. Sam's executive team, the

program manager and chief architect, would be in supportive, not controlling, roles. A network of six middle managers would be formed specifically to deliver Rapid. They would be accountable to one another, to Sam, and to the company.

Sam has found his second transformational idea, and Abe has seen the diverge-converge cycle in action.

Chapter 8

Intentional Networks— Engage the Middle

Prior to the PC revolution, operating systems (OS) were huge complex beasts full of walled-off source code. This all changed in 1987 when Andrew Tanenbaum, in Amsterdam, published a UNIX operating system clone called MINIX. Across the pond in the US, Richard Stallman (MIT) published the code for GNU. Building on these, a young Finnish student, Linus Torvalds, created a new operating system that grew to become the only real contender to Microsoft's OS. How and why did this happen?

When Torvalds published his OS code he invited others to use *and modify* it as they saw fit, an invitation neither Tanenbaum nor Stallman considered. Additionally, "Linux," Torvalds' brainchild, could be used commercially, spawning a rapidly growing global network of users and entrepreneurs (Red Hat being the poster child). Linux still has no official organizational home, yet it remains a leading OS for web servers and is used by Dell, HP, and IBM in their PC businesses.

"That's software," you say, "but business is different: Loosely coupled networks and communities won't work in corporate settings." True, organizational networks, communities of practice, and software communities are built on relationships, not corporate mandate, and for that reason it is hard to see how social networks can also generate economic returns that impact the corporate bottom line. But we've found that turning the middle managers in your company into a robust network, an information and collaboration highway, has the ability to directly impact your business outcomes.

To see how this is possible, let's look at three companies in which researchers Rob Cross and Robert J. Thomas leveraged manager networks to generate growth and performance.[1] Along the way we will use their findings to learn how to apply networks to build a hybrid organization (Figure 2.1).

Halliburton, our first example, is a global provider of products and services to the petroleum and energy industries. It was Halliburton's desire to strategically design organizational networks capable of producing measurable results directly linked to corporate goals and financial performance. Cross and Thomas worked with them, using organizational network analysis (ONA), to deploy 19 *intentional* networks across various business units and technical services with the intent of finding solutions—such as cost and time saving methods for drilling wells—that could be replicated across the globe.

One network, composed of engineers who complete the drilling and begin production, focused on designing solutions for individual

---

1 Rob Cross and Robert J. Thomas, *Driving Results Through Social Networks: How Top Organizations Leverage Networks for Performance and Growth* (San Francisco, Jossey-Bass, 2009).

wells. Working as a global network, they were able to resolve an issue with a deep water well in West Africa in just a day by tapping into a virtual forum and individual specialists. *Moreover,* that solution was reapplied over the next 24 hours to three other wells across the globe! Halliburton's continuing efforts to transfer knowledge and encourage collaboration using intentional networks increased revenues 22 percent, lowered the cost of poor quality by 66 percent, improved productivity 10 percent, and decreased customer dissatisfaction ratings by 24 percent *in one year.*[2]

In this example Halliburton was faced with a dynamic environment that *required* collaboration and cooperation between decentralized engineers across a diverse set of circumstances and constraints—very similar to the conditions that enterprises making the digital journey encounter, conditions ripe for solutions by an intentional network of middle managers. Engaging the middle of your organization as a network allows you to apply targeted actions to multiple sites during transformation, uncover structural holes and silos that are slowing adoption and knowledge transfer, and better use the knowledge of subject matter experts and positive deviants.

Another example, this one involving a global financial services company, also shows how time and money are saved when information, resources, and expertise flow across the network. Cross and Thomas worked with executives to improve the connectivity of project managers (PMs) across this company. The end result? PMs working locally as information brokers improved their collaboration by analyzing their networks (using ONA), which produced an aggregated *monthly* savings of 3,383 hours or approximately $215,000 (based on average loaded FTE costs). While this was an interesting outcome, executives were actually more interested in

---

2 Ibid, p. 71.

synergies that might result from cross-unit collaboration, using PMs as boundary spanners.

To improve the ability of the network to create synergies, flow information, and collaborate across boundaries, key information brokers were asked to engage with one person outside their local network. This yielded $140,000/year in savings and added $865,000 in returns generated by cross-unit collaboration.[3]

This relatively small investment of time and effort created relational bridges that closed structural holes and improved information flow. Imagine similarly linking up middle managers throughout your company to create synergies, reduce redundant costs, and flow information during digital transformation. Think of how that would also strengthen and speed up the dynamics of change at the local level as managers learn from each other how to apply the practices of digital.

Finally, an example of networks being used to discover and remove collaborative inefficiencies caused by outdated role definition in an IT department: The CIO of a leading utility sought to understand how collaboration across four architecture roles (application, business, data, and infrastructure) impacted decisions and efficiency. Cross and Thomas assessed collaboration as the interaction time spent between the four architecture roles and converted it to cost per role. They found that each role spent most of their time interacting with each other, which isn't surprising, and that the amount of time they spent with other roles in collaboration varied widely. This finding is similar to functional managers working in a product development team within a business unit.

What was most interesting was the role-dependent cost of collaboration, the cost of interactions across the roles measured as employees'

---

3 Ibid. Pp. 72-74.

time. The most costly role overall, based on time and dollars, was that of infrastructure architects—who spent most of their time interacting with each other, setting the technical direction for the whole department. But based on collaboration, the most costly roles were data and business unit architects, who spent the majority of their time working with the other three roles. This emphasized the need for social skills along with technical skills for these two roles. Additionally data and business unit architects were the smallest teams, significantly outnumbered by application and infrastructure architects, perhaps causing the excessive need to collaborate and suggesting the need to better balance the allocation of resources. The CIO used these findings to turn the role of infrastructure architect into a boundary spanning role, using their greater numbers and involving them early and often in the work of the others.[4]

This last study is of particular interest, as it illustrates that the nature of roles, particularly those in the middle of the organization, changes dramatically during digital transformation. As agile teams and engaged product owners are established in Waves 1 and 2, the connectivity they provide removes the need for roles that managers have previously provided. What to do with these roles, often middle managers, is how we shift from a simple hierarchy to a hybrid organizational model (hierarchy and network).

HIDDEN VALUE IN THE MIDDLE OF YOUR COMPANY

Years ago Andrew Grove wrote that "Middle managers are the muscle and bone of every sizable organization, no matter how loose or 'flattened' the hierarchy, but they are largely ignored despite their immense importance to our society and economy."[5] He was on to something;

---

4 Ibid. Pp. 83-88.

5 Andrew Grove, *High Output Management* (New York: Vintage Books, 1995).

unfortunately his warning was not heeded, for today coordination and decision-making in large corporations remains painful and slow *because* issues are typically run up the human flagpole and back down through layers of middle managers, whose jobs in current bureaucratic corporations are essentially useless. They just slow things down.

Of course there isn't a large enterprise that can avoid functioning as a multilevel organization. Yet there is a misplaced desire to make hierarchy the enemy of agility. Rather, it is bureaucracy that is the enemy. Hierarchy exists in all healthy ecosystems, where information and authority flow in all directions. During the shift to digital, top-down bureaucracy must atrophy while nested hierarchies of lateral and middle control naturally thrive. In fact, daily or immediate control and decision-making needs to move to the base of the hierarchy, which allows the top and center to be more deliberate and have a medium- to long-term strategic perspective.

Removing bureaucracy is solved by designing *intentional networks* across management that connect the company using information brokers and boundary spanners. It is clear, based on research and anecdotes — not to mention logic — that human networks enable the flow of ideas and information by connecting people to each other. And the financial value of these networks, such as those cited above, have been repeatedly validated across companies and industries. And yet most large enterprises seem to lack the means to intentionally design and nurture these networks. One has to wonder: Where is the chief network officer?

In the late 1990s corporate knowledge and innovation experts Ikujiro Nonaka and Hirotaka Takeuchi developed a management strategy they called *Middle-Up-Down*. Their research led them to propose what they called a "hypertext" organizational structure: a combination of network and hierarchy that allows loosely coupled teams to self-organize across business units — which increases their ability to collaborate and create business value. Ironically, Nonaka and Takeuchi are more remembered in the agile community for their *Harvard Business Review* article on high-performing Scrum teams than they are for their paradigm-shifting organizational design that provides a new and critical role for middle managers in companies seeking business agility. But in moving to digital, we can not only see this other value and give Nonaka and Takeuchi their due on that count . . . but fully utilize it to create the hybrid organizational model we need in Wave 3 (Figure 2.1).

Most of us are familiar with the concept of hypertext, even if we don't know the technology behind it. In essence, it provides the user with access to multiple layers of stored files, text, and media (e.g., video). The core feature of hypertext, and one we want to use in organizational design, is the ability to move in and out of different content and context environments. From the organizational design perspective, this produces multiple interconnected structures that the company can use depending on the situation.

Imagine a product development ecosystem that uses a hierarchy for things like finance, performance/HR management, and maintaining a product backlog, data, and infrastructure. Nested within the hierarchy are product development networks composed of managers, teams, SMEs, communities of practice, etc. Members of the product development network operate in both these structures, taking advantage of characteristics of each as they adapt to the dynamics of their business.

Taking the lead from Nonaka and Takeuchi's *Middle-Up-Down management,* we have found that creating a variation of hypertext organization can revamp the role of middle manager and reinvigorate collaboration and innovation, particularly across boundaries. Before we describe *how* to transform the middle of your organization, let's talk about the outcome we are seeking.

Recall that in Chapter 7 we talked about the need for horizontal links to successfully complete complex, innovative work. Middle managers, working as a horizontal network, provide this by encouraging collaboration, coordination, and innovation and making visible and actionable the gap between executive vision (Middle-Up) and the reality of execution (Middle-Down). They act as boundary spanners, connecting individuals across boundaries, *and* as information brokers, encouraging collaboration and cooperation within product development groups (see sidebar).

Using frameworks like Helix, business and technology middle managers become knowledge engineers who create economic value, turning market signals into meaningful ideas and insights that are

Managers fill the value creation void in the middle of most large enterprises by:

~ Becoming highly skilled product managers who are in contact with key customers.

~ Being able to generate and test hypotheses that innovate existing products and explore new concepts and ideas.

~ Expanding their dedicated knowledge to become "specializing generalists" capable of leading diverse T-Shaped or feature teams.

~ Encouraging dialogue and communication across teams and functional boundaries.

~ Engendering trust through establishing a safe working environment and healthy social physics.

~ Providing a vision of the future without ignoring learning from the past.

acted on to produce products and services that customers value. Throughout we have argued that corporate agility requires that bureaucracy be removed and replaced with a healthy ecosystem. Our modification of Nonaka and Takeuchi's hypertext organization provides large corporations a both/and solution: both a hierarchy (but not a bureaucracy) and a network — an ecosystem that utilizes the beneficial attributes of both.

Middle-Up-Down, operationalized as a middle manager network, generates a continuous flow of information that allows the company to adapt to internal changes as well as changes in the market ecosystem. It places middle managers at the intersection of both *vertical and horizontal* flows of information, knowledge, and work, where they can have their most positive impact on strategy and operations. Combining hierarchy and networks not only eliminates bureaucracy, it also allows us to take advantage of some important strategic paradoxes: efficiency and flexibility, standardization and variability, rule-based vs. complex adaptive processes, to name a few. Viewing hierarchy and network as complementary and synergistic organizational structures, rather than as mutually exclusive, enables organization agility.

The properly functioning middle manager network, formal and informal, encourages open interactions between people and the sharing of tacit and explicit knowledge, which are used for decision-making, resource allocation, governance, and authority.

CREATING THE MIDDLE NETWORK

Hierarchies perform well during periods of stability, providing predictability and standardization to business leaders, but there is a risk during these periods that bureaucracy will reassert itself. To maintain a healthy hierarchy, without *too much* order and structure, especially in the areas of strategy, governance, and leadership, we build "intentional networks." These are particularly valuable during periods of disruption and VUCA (volatility, uncertainty, complexity, and ambiguity), when hierarchy needs the flexibility of networks to survive. It helps transformational leaders to understand this oscillation between hierarchy and network, which positions the company at the edge of chaos, by appreciating that a hierarchy is simply a form of network, one that is pulled vertically by a single node. Then, if we connect all these single nodes into a network that crosses organizational boundaries and functions, we end up with an intentional middle manager network.

When designing a middle manager network, we want it to be flexible, dynamic, participatory, and adaptive (see sidebar). This requires a light touch — few rules, self-management, self-governance, and self-organization. Networks easily accommodate to the diversity that exists across large enterprises, they adapt to stringent time requirements (i.e., urgency) and the need to focus on a well-defined outcome, and their information and knowledge flow capitalize on product synergies. This makes them particularly useful for product development

Network structures in organizations tend to be:

~ Horizontal, dynamic, and fluid; making them difficult to contain and regulate.

~ Supportive of both subject matter experts and diverse points of view.

~ Able to socialize and share knowledge and ideas rapidly.

~ Composed of empowered, autonomous people and teams; able to self-manage, self-govern, and self-organize.

~ Capable of reaching outside the company to build relationships with customers, providing rich feedback.

teams working in complex, cross-organizational environments. Networks are also capable of overcoming constraints in innovative ways, making use of distributed, often tacit, knowledge. They are, however, lacking in their ability to store, maintain, and update corporate knowledge over time. For this we need our hierarchy.

Designing and establishing a middle manager network requires that you encourage and have active participation. A healthy middle network starts with local management and organically expands by attracting managers from across the organization. Working together, the middle manager network unearths and exposes the contradictions and constraints generated by the reality of product development. They then work with executives and strategic leaders to resolve these (a Middle-Up action) or innovate by working *on* the organization (perhaps a Helix cycle). For example, when middle managers realize that strategy needs to change, they elevate challenges and opportunities to the executive team for consideration. Once the strategy is clarified, they flow that information *vertically* to autonomous delivery teams (i.e., Middle-Down) and *horizontally* to align the whole company (using horizontal partners to connect to other networks).

The collaboration between executives and the middle network results in an *agreement* on the outcomes while preserving the network's ability to *determine* the means of achieving them (a diverge-converge cycle). And, because the middle network creates horizontal links between managers (via their role as boundary spanners), product development teams become more aware of organizational synergies as well as how to repair relationships, such as accidental adversaries and systemically produced conflict.

The network of middle managers improves the ability of key result champions to find and enroll horizontal partners across the organization. It also promotes conversation within the product ecosystem that drives collaboration and coordinates workflow. In this way the middle network can, at the very least, respond to challenges and opportunities, make better and more strategic decisions, coordinate use of budgets, and quickly manage scheduling gaps. All of these produce innovative ways to operationalize corporate strategy. Of course this middle manager network does not emerge without encouragement and support from the company's top leaders. With that in mind, if there's one message you take away from this discussion, we hope it's this: *Your middle managers are critical to your successful transformation across the digital waves.*

Let's examine three ways that executives can start revitalizing the middle and create their most effective middle network.

First, focus on outcomes, not deliverables. The need to remove bureaucracy is real and pressing. You must do this to get past Wave 1. We believe that the executive's role is to help middle managers understand the *outcomes* they are seeking, then let them work together to collectively figure out how to accomplish them. Under these conditions the middle becomes a flexible, responsive network, held jointly accountable and capable of doing whatever is necessary, even down to making trade-offs and compromises, to move the company forward.

Middle managers are subject matter experts with knowledge, experience, and networks they have been developing for years. They understand the current reality. Together, they have a holistic view of the diverse parts of product development, and they know what is and what isn't working. These managers are poised to work with teams to achieve strategic outcomes and share resources, ideas, knowledge. And, utilizing each manager's personal networks, they can recruit expertise and experience from across the company.

Without revitalizing your middle managers, without seeing them as crucial assets, you are ignoring a human network that knows how to innovate *and* how to get work done. Flattening the company must first make it more horizontally connected.

Second, do what only you can do. To begin revitalizing the middle management layers, you must provide people new roles and a new purpose.
In essence, say, "You're valuable to the teams below you, to the executives above you, and to all the other people with whom you interact
in the organization. How can you best achieve that value collectively
rather than individually?" Find challenges your middle manager network can take on to drive your digital transformation. Encourage
them to work *in and on* the organization as agents of transformation.

Facing the turbulence of transforming to digital, middle manager
networks become the force that forms a "strategic knot"[6] that links
top management to agile product development teams. They make
sense of chaotic conditions and find transformational ideas that drive
innovation and creativity. Many middle managers tell us that, for
them to be more effective, they need to learn how to coach, to work
across boundaries, and to become more strategic and business focused.
Rather than being the clay layer, an impediment to both transparency
and the flow of information, middle managers *want* to play a new role,
a better, more involved, more productive role. And they can become
that *information layer*, sharing resources and spreading learning.

Third, openly utilize the social platform that communities and networks establish.
Middle manager networks act as social platforms on which work
gets done. As an ecosystem, the social platform, curated by the
middle manager network, draws upon the expertise of the whole
organization. Being able to jump across the organization to find the
right people and the right technology to solve thorny problems and
turn failure into value creation is the task of the network. It enables
individuals and teams to sense and respond to a rapidly evolving

---

6 Ikujiro Nonaka and Hirotaka Takeuchi, *The Knowledge-Creating Company: How
    Japanese Companies Create the Dynamics of Innovation* (New York: Oxford University
    Press, 1995), 128.

market ecosystem. The middle manager network can access the whole company and even stretch into the external world, encouraging partners to participate. This results in higher performance, in the ability to turn data into knowledge, and to transform weak signals into experiments and innovations.

The middle of every company is composed of managers who have social connections to different parts of the corporation. They stand in the structural holes between people, functions, and groups that are not connected, and they connect them. This produces one of the most powerful characteristics of human networks: reciprocity. The middle's social capital harnesses the power of reciprocity, attracting the resources and knowledge that managers need today by promising to repay the favor to the network in the future. To access the reciprocity of the network, we ask: Whom do you know who can . . . ? This utilizes the well-known concept of "six degrees of separation"; within six singular connections one can access the whole organization. And it works just as one would think it does:

When the middle network is stumped, needs critical information or resources, or needs someone to be a horizontal champion for an amazing KR, members reach out to their immediate network. But if that doesn't provide what they need, they ask: Who *in your network* might be able to help? In this way a small group can generate rather quickly a huge network of people they may not directly know, but who can, and will, help them, always receiving a warm handoff as they go. And the value they are creating as the network expands and contracts is technical, adaptive, and social.

THE WELL-CONNECTED COMPANY

So what exactly does the middle *do* to contribute to your digital transformation or the work of product development? How do they accomplish all these grand things?

To get started, middle managers must work on themselves—identifying and clarifying their own underlying assumptions, mental models, and leadership skills—and it is best if they undertake this work as a group, which enables them to determine how to influence others. All successful transformations require middle managers to spend time in conversation and retrospection, exploring their collective differences and similarities and becoming a force for change. Together they need to examine how norms, culture, and social memes are impeding or advancing their success. They learn together and coach each other, and then they teach and coach others.

Middle managers are central to operationalizing and executing the digital strategy, reducing risk, and creating safe-to-fail experiments. Corporate and business strategies, generated by top executives, are aspirational but often vague. Operationalizing the strategy needs to be actionable and is going to look and feel different across the company's many business environments. The middle network works to turn corporate strategy into appropriate local activities, reinforcing intent and at the same time respecting on-the-ground context and conditions. It is the old adage, "think global, act local" in action.

Middle management can and should be the means of closing the gap between the espoused and the practiced strategy. Once goals are set, the middle manager network holds people accountable and gives them the power to act, the power to become owners of outcomes. Being accountable and having the power to act is also indispensable for the middle network, which must determine what to measure, how to measure, and how to report progress to those above and below them (Middle-Up-Down).

Once established, the middle network becomes the primary group in the company to experiment *in* and *on* the organization. They teach the hypotheses testing and good experimentation practices that are essential to technical, product, and adaptive transformations. When frameworks like Helix and Strive are used by the middle manager network, operationalizing the digital transformation strategy through experimentation and execution becomes woven together with the shift to being customer and product focused.

The middle network is how exploration and experimentation deliver the highest return on learning. Carefully crafted experiments can be undertaken to preemptively address volatility, uncertainty, complexity, and ambiguity (VUCA) in the company and market, which allows resolution of it. As the middle network learns to turn VUCA into increased vigilance, understanding, containment, and agility, your ability to change and pivot locally and globally increases greatly.

Similarly, middle manager networks can turn constraints into constructive tension to foster innovation. Constraints always exist, but middle networks—because of their diversity—understand them better than teams do. Middle managers ensure that the right constraints are addressed and that the tough questions are asked and answered. Collectively the network learns to negotiate and make trade-offs, interpreting situations in a way that engages all stakeholders, keeping the organization aligned vertically and horizontally.

For example, one corporation we worked with had two distinct but synergistic technical platforms, one addressing marketing and one addressing customer service interactions. They showed what is becoming a classic choice in the digital business world: They could remain organized under a single leader, a tightly coupled hierarchical organizational design, to take advantage of their synergies; or they could be loosely coupled, linked by their middle manager networks and encouraged to learn and collaborate—to reduce redundancies and make optimal use of knowledge and resources, but without the added structural overhead. The network structure in cases like this allows for a lean organizational structure, creates more agility, and reduces the need for reorganization during transformation.

Middle manager networks replace directives with conversations and coaching. Collectively they ask tough questions and decide who to enroll to solve them. As these networks change their role and leadership style, people are encouraged to push hard on ideas, data, and information, rather than one another.

As we've said before, there's no single game plan for moving from hierarchy to network to ecosystem. When faced with this kind of transformational challenge, we need everyone to bring all of their experience to bear on making the journey. Revitalizing the middle is about letting talented managers work on what matters to them, and to everyone else. Through coaching self-managing teams and designing organizational transformation, their interest and curiosity are engaged and their work becomes meaningful in new ways.

When middle management functions as a network, rather than a hierarchy, everything from product design to planning to decision-making evolves. Inside the network, human relationships and interactions form a social platform for addressing complex organizational challenges and opportunities. Networks develop across functional boundaries, disrupting and replacing silos with personal connections that allow managers to identify and resolve sensitive adaptive issues.

A strong middle manager network establishes the building blocks for the ecosystems you'll need in Wave 3, and the first building block is creating the middle manager network. Removing the impermeable clay layer of traditional middle management is building block two, preparing the organization for linking technology to business and where functional silos collapse. In Wave 3 the middle manager network provides coordination and control for a loosely coupled, autonomous ecosystem of microbusinesses capable of interacting with the external market, partners, and customers.

Of course no company transforms all at once, but an engaged, networked middle can pull the organization forward, working on local problems and complex issues: How do we move to the cloud? What do we need to do to automate this process? What skills and knowledge do we need to fulfill this customer need? The middle is the network that manages the transformation, keeping others informed and mobilized, guiding the cycles of testing, adapting, pivoting, and learning. That's the power of the revitalized middle.

At times, empowering the middle within your organization can feel like you are operating on trust alone. But to move forward, you have to trust that the path you're taking will lead you to a new way of working, benefitting from using two structures — a hierarchy, yes, but only in concert with a network — instead of one.

INTENTIONAL NETWORKS RECAP

"Creating the middle" is likely the most important thing you can do to transform your organization and its culture. The building blocks that intentionally transform the middle make up a cultural algorithm of leadership that produces new ways of interacting with employees, customers, and the market. These establish a culture of safety, experimentation, and innovation.

Middle managers can solve problems rapidly because the network is integrated and collegial. Collectively, middle managers identify and remove bottlenecks, allocate existing or scarce resources, and creatively address constraints. The middle network keeps an eye on what's going on, providing multidirectional flow of information, which doesn't exist in a hierarchy alone.

Like any healthy ecosystem, a healthy middle manager network is diverse. Assembling the middle builds diversity of thought, function, and experience into your organization. People in the network bring together multiple points of view, solutions, and experiences. And because the network crosses organizational and functional boundaries, managers bring a holistic perspective to local experimentation and innovation.

A reanimated middle drives digital transformation. As you navigate the technological waves, the human and product development systems must—and will—adapt to match the changing flow of work from customers to agile teams. The middle manager network provides a social and knowledge platform that enables the transformation of the company. This is the magic of the middle.

KEY TAKEAWAYS: INTENTIONAL NETWORKS

Executives:

Revitalizing the middle is about letting talented managers work on what matters to them, and to everyone else. Make sure your middle managers understand the *outcomes* you are seeking, then let them work together to collectively figure out how to accomplish them. Find challenges your middle manager network can take on to drive your digital transformation. Encourage them to work in *and* on the organization as agents of transformation. Educate your middle managers to be information brokers and boundary spanners, then task them to solve critical technical and adaptive challenges.

Transformation Leaders:

Middle managers are core to operationalizing and executing the digital strategy, reducing risk, and creating safe-to-fail experiments. The collaboration between executives and the middle network results in an *agreement* on the outcomes of transformation, yet preserves the ability to influence the activities the network uses to achieve them. Your role as network designer causes the middle network to organically expand and attract managers from across the organization.

Managers:

You are responsible for flowing information and working across the whole organizational system. With your peers, you operationalize strategy, guide the performance of teams, and provide flexible, local coordination and collaboration. As technical experts, your networks uncover the root cause of problems and provide holistic, systemic fixes. Middle managers must work on themselves, personally and as a collective, by identifying and clarifying their own underlying assumptions, mental models, and leadership skills. Digital transformation and the middle network are your developmental plan for the foreseeable future.

Employees:

Middle manager networks are there to work with you to become self-managing, self-governing, and self-organizing. They provide outcomes, resources, ideas, and knowledge. Through their personal networks they can find the expertise and experience you need to achieve your objectives and key results. Use your managers to establish horizontal connections, new relationships, and collaborations. And use their networks to remove contradictions and constraints generated by the reality of digital product development.

INTERMEZZO
Abe's All Hands on Deck

Abe stands in front of the crowd, facing the telepresence camera and surrounded by graphs and charts depicting lines of growth and bars of capacity. He is nervous about this presentation, his first to his whole organization since he kicked off the digital transformation six months ago. Much has been accomplished, but even more remains to be done. Today is his opportunity to enlist his whole organization along with his business partners as he delivers his vision of the future, the transformational journey that he wants to take them all on.

In the back row sit his mentors, Anna, Ethan, and Gina. On the stage with him are Sam, now two months into an amazing turnaround of the Rapid program, and Nancy. Nancy is representing a cross-sectional group of employees who have been studying the organization and who will be presenting for the first time their strategy recommendations for a digital transformation. In the front row sits Abe's leadership team, all onboard and ready to lead the charge to the future. Scattered throughout the audience are business leaders and executives, who Abe invited to hear what he has to say in order to encourage their participation

Abe clears his throat and steps forward. The room quiets.

"Let me start by telling you how I got here today. It all started with a lunch meeting with colleagues of mine from other companies; we plan these once each quarter." Abe tells the story of his journey since that fateful day, how much he has learned about transformation from Gina, Anna, and Ethan.

"As you all see," he says, "the props I have always used during these all-hands meetings are still here." As he walks towards the charts, he continues, "But they are here today so that you can watch as I personally jettison them," while, in an overly dramatic way, he flings the things off their stands one by one! A moment of stunned silence ensues before the audience roars in approval.

"Before today, I needed these to talk to you. I needed them to try to tell you a story, maybe motivate you to change and to transform the way we work and how we partner with our businesses. But I no longer need these . . . because I have discovered that you all already know what we need to do to transform. Before realizing this I worried that I had to carry the whole burden, make all the decisions, and be the smartest guy in the room. You all remember that Abe, I'm sure.

"Well, he is gone; up and left the company. In his place you now have a colleague who appreciates all the talent and energy that every one of you brings to the company. On paper I'll be leading this transformation, but we all know that it is really a daily activity, a new way of working for all of us, and not a plan I'm going to roll out. I want you to understand that I will likely get confused, make mistakes, and get anxious about the journey . . . just like you. I tell you this because I am fairly certain that you will experience something similar, that these feelings are natural, and that we're all in this together.

"But that's the good news: The journey we are taking is *ours* to make. It is not the product of off-site management meeting or external consultants. What you'll likely find most interesting — if a little scary — is the kind of journey this will be . . . something much different than you've even imagined, but what is needed to make our way in today's digital world.

"Let me introduce this new direction by telling you that, first, this is a journey that has no destination — for it comes as a result of much broader, ongoing changes in our markets. That's why we are not going to have a big launch. We are not going to roll out a finished transformation plan; heck, we are already in the midst of it! We are going to scale organically, with our business partners, in product cohorts that are customer-centric. Our customers have created our success thus far, and they continue to determine our future success. Their priorities must always be our priorities."

From both the business and technology perspectives, Abe gets down to details, sketching out particularly the problems the company may face in delivering customer value at the current pace of change in the market. He acknowledges that some in the organization will be skeptical, may even assume there is a hidden agenda behind his words. He anticipates their concerns, and assures them that this isn't the case, that downsizing and working oneself out of a job is *not* part of the process.

"But," he says, "some of you will find our new way of working so different that you may *choose* to move on . . . and that is okay. We hope, instead, that you will choose to work in this new way and find your place in it, for the key to our success is universal involvement in the process. If we are going to reinvent the way we work together and produce value that our customers recognize, we all have to participate. The most powerful ideas are going to come from those of you doing the work that is closest to our customers. That means that the processes and management structure that we have built up over the years need to change. I want to acknowledge that what I am suggesting we do will shake up the political power and bureaucratic fiefdoms that exist today."

Totally unexpectedly, the room breaks out in spontaneous applause. Abe is startled. Then he begins to smile. He thought he would have to convince them. Now he realizes they didn't need to be convinced . . . they need something meaningful to do, something that will make a difference.

At the height of acceptance of this new plan, Abe realizes it is of the *plan,* not of him. It is time to turn things over to Nancy, to illustrate that it is not the upper echelon of the company who will be running the show.

Nancy is a middle manager whose name kept coming up as Abe moved around the organization. After he learned about transformation, Abe realized that he needed a collective vision of the future, one that everyone could rally around. He asked Nancy to form a cross-organizational team to explore, through interviews and local focus groups, the ideal way of working together from the employee's perspective. He encouraged Nancy to spend as much time with business people as she did with technologists, and that is precisely what Nancy achieved.

Nancy presents the findings of her team and their recommendations for a digital transformation strategy, including a drafted mission statement and set of values for the whole organization to finalize. When she concludes, the room again erupts in applause.

"Clearly," Abe says, picking up the thread as the applause dies down, "we have some significant changes to make to achieve the vision that Nancy's team has set for us. To initiate these changes, I suggest . . . but do not mandate"—laughter and sporadic clapping encourage Abe to chuckle—"that teams get together and work out ways they can locally implement these recommendations in their daily work. Let's give ourselves a couple of months to make these ideas a living reality. Anyone with an idea or a revision to the recommendations, vision, and values . . . just speak up."

"I have an idea," someone in the middle of the audience shouts out.

"Let's hear it," Abe responds.

"Let's turn finalization of Nancy's recommendations into workshops, so that we get to know the whole organization and appreciate the diverse ideas and knowledge we collectively have." The speaker continues, suddenly self-conscious, "I'm not sure if that is a good idea or if we could afford it or make it happen . . . but . . . " His voice trails off.

"It's a great idea!" Abe says, "In fact, it fits right in."

"Boy, are you lucky," someone shouts. People around the room laugh. This is the wildest, most "accepting" all-hands Abe has ever been part of.

"I have been thinking about how to leverage ideas just like that," Abe says. "To encourage experimentation and innovation with our products, our processes, and our organizational structure, I want to set up Design Boards. My idea is to use some of the discretionary funds I have to finance new ideas through the proof-of-concept phase. Anyone who has something they think is worthy needs to gather enough support, cross-organizationally, as Nancy's team did, and present it to them for consideration." Abe turns to Nancy. "It looks as if we have our first candidate."

Next Abe invites Sam up to tell his story about the turnaround of the Rapid program. Sam speaks passionately about how six middle managers had taken a struggling initiative, worth millions to the company, and, by operating as a network, pulled it together. "They are on track to deliver their commitments by the end of the year," he says. Sam admits to his own early skepticism. However, after seeing the results, he also turned his direct reports into a leadership network so that he could focus on things *only he could do*. "Abe taught me that phrase," Sam concludes.

"That is a great segue into what I want to say next," Abe says. "Success in this new world we are creating depends on our ability to establish and nurture relationships. Our products require strong relationships with our business partners and customers, but we also need a way to create relationships across the organization so that we can learn, develop, and grow together. To do this, I have been investigating a new management and performance evaluation. Since everyone in this room has to deal with the latter, let me start there. I have just started working with our head of human resources and proposed that we eliminate the nine-box ranking system."

People applaud and whistle.

Abe goes on, "If we want people to learn fast and experiment, we need to become less risk averse. We can't change the constraints that working within the financial sector imposes, and these should actually help us be more creative, but we can encourage a more entrepreneurial mindset as we make this transformational journey. In fact, we need that.

"We have to accept that we don't know what changes we need to make or exactly how to make those changes. We have some tools and frameworks we can use to design and implement smart experiments and fast feedback loops. But I want to be clear with you all . . . what I thought at the start was an adoption of lean-agile practices is really an organizational transformation, and nothing less. Those practices and tools are helpful, but they are not the answer. The upshot: This could get messy. We are rewiring our part of the company from bureaucratic, command-and-control silos to an ecosystem of interrelated equals. Everything is up for grabs. And we can't take ten years to do this. But the potential upside is undeniable; in fact, I think it is inevitable.

"So let's get started. First we are going to ask managers to take on the roles of strategists and transformation agents, because my executive team has things to do that only we can do, things like orchestrating the integration between technology and our business colleagues, and determining our strategic direction for the next year or two. We need to set a few critical goals that we all march toward as we write our objectives and key results. We need to make sure that corporate functions like HR, finance, and centralized planning change with us without slowing us down. And we need to better understand our customers and the experience they expect to have with all the products we provide them."

Abe breathes a sigh of satisfaction. He pauses to appreciate the group that he has working for him, with him. "If everyone in this room isn't on board by now — or at least excited about the possibilities," Abe concludes, "then I haven't done my job. And if you are wondering what to do next, check your email. You will have received a transformation playbook that gets us all started on the same page. It has some new language that we are going to use. Nancy's story and Sam's story are both in there. And there is a description, which I think you will all relate to, of how we have discovered that change and transformation are happening today. There are also a couple of frameworks we can use to get started to perform well-designed experiments. I want to invite anyone who wants to play a larger role in our transformation to contact me personally and immediately, because there is a lot to do.

"Thank you all for your attention, enthusiasm — and willingness to add your considerable talents to the exciting journey we are only just beginning."

Chapter 9

Leading Digital— Chart Your Course

There is no single exemplary story of digital leadership. Few traditional enterprises have made this journey, although many are well on their way. It is an act of leading in a new way because digital transformation involves simultaneous business, technology, and organizational change. As we see from Abe's journey, moving to digital is bigger than adopting lean-agile techniques and practices, and it emphasizes the ability to re-role yourself and others. Letting go of the company's historical successes, as well as your own, means jettisoning many of the activities that have defined leadership in the past. Following Abe's journey, we begin to appreciate, as he did, that he was as much a part of the problem as he was a key to the solution. This is the challenge for all executives and leaders—to recognize that you may be, first, the obstacle, but then must become the beacon to successful digital transformation.

Countless books have been written on leadership, many devoted to great business leaders from the past. These stories contain valuable leadership lessons, but we live in different times, faster times, more dynamic times. The challenges these leaders encountered were real and pressing for them in their time, but the forces at play then required a very different mindset, a different style of engagement, than leaders need today. Today's digital terrain is composed of markets in rapid flux, markets that produce radical change that create both challenge *and* opportunity. We think that leading the digital transformation requires viewing "leadership" as a verb rather than a noun . . . *the act of leading.*

LEADING DIGITAL TRANSFORMATION: ACTIONS, BEHAVIORS, AND SKILLS

As we've seen, leading any transformation, and particularly a digital transformation, means you can't rely only on the skills and knowledge you have developed over your career; nor are the behaviors and skills you need taught in B-school or weekend executive programs. Suddenly you need to become a student again, you must adopt a beginner's mindset and be willing to learn from anyone and everyone. Abe's dialogues in our Intermezzos were largely generated by our interviews and work with technology and business leaders across many industries. The first — and probably most important — thing most of them realized is that their transformation as leaders is the cornerstone of larger corporate transformation.

This makes the work highly personal . . . and often deeply disruptive. In any era, a fundamental aspect of leading is being self-aware, not caught up in the past and not trying to be someone else, even someone you admire. How much you need to change, and can change, determines how much the company can change.

Research from the MIT Initiative on the Digital Economy/Capgemini Consulting found that digital transformation required leaders, especially executives, to become active boundary spanners within their companies and their markets. The research showed that nondigital-native enterprises must invest in both technical capability and leadership capability to realize the benefits of digital. When they did, they were 26 percent more profitable (EBIT Margin and Net Profit Margin) and generated 9 percent higher revenues per employee than companies that focused on only one capability, leadership *or* technology. [1]

These are significant gains, but just the beginning when we consider what a digital transformation can offer corporations. McKinsey researchers Lowell Bryan and Claudia Joyce found that thinking-intensive companies were able to create new wealth, as measured by net income and market capitalization, by deriving value from the seemingly intangible asset of the minds of their employees. An increase in net income generated per employee, which came from the company's ability to utilize their employees' ideas, decisions, knowledge, and relationships, significantly increased corporate profits. It allowed these companies to overcome the organizational complexity that all large enterprises face. Yet only 2 percent of the top 1,500 public companies examined were taking advantage of this hidden and underutilized asset.[2]

Achieving corporate agility means embedding the knowledge and skills for self-management, self-governance, and self-organization, which requires redefining the roles of manager and leader.

---

1 George Westerman, Didier Bonnet, and Andrew McAfee, *Leading Digital* (Boston: HBR Publishing, 2014).

2 Lowell Bryan and Claudia Joyce, *Mobilizing Minds: Creating Wealth from Talent in the 21ˢᵗ-Century Organization* (New York: McGraw Hill, 2007).

To embed self-management, leaders must provide guidance and set constraints, ask powerful questions, and encourage people to be thorough and rigorous in their experimentation. Self-governance requires a higher level of community, collaboration, and coordination than most companies have today. Leading here must ensure that these communities have the time and skills to effectively govern themselves. Finally, self-organization means that teams have—and use—the information about customers, markets, and technology they need to make good decisions. Self-organization assumes that autonomy is in the organization's best interest and that people working at the customer interface are valuable contributors capable of addressing even the most complex business challenges.

GENERATING THE CONDITIONS FOR TRANSFORMATION

There is no "best" way, no silver bullet framework, no standard journey for successful digital transformation. Every company and every business within it is a living system, a community of people full of talent and ideas. If you are "in charge" of the transformation to digital, then view every action you take as an experiment, and don't let anyone tell you "their solution" should be applied to the whole organization. When you aren't hearing conversations about horizontal collaboration and collective interaction that are driving new ideas, and you aren't being asked really tough questions, it's time to start leading differently.

And you are not leading at all if you're working alone. Effective leadership spawns deep emotional commitment from your colleagues, who are essentially volunteering to join in and cocreate the future with you. Leading happens when your interactions with others offer them connection, purpose, and a deep sense of ownership. This means every conversation you have as a leader is strategic.

Leading transformation means you are holding the organization at the edge of chaos — where order and disorder are both present and their tension drives creativity and innovation. This often takes leaders out of their personal and professional comfort zone, creating your learning agenda. Transformation requires leaders to create environments that invite inclusion and encourage diversity (Figure 9.1). Leading in these situations arises from an inner drive to build things and grow people, to tinker and to learn by doing. It requires leaders to see through the mess and find clarity — to invite the right stakeholders into the conversation.

Inclusivity and participation expands the conversation, inviting multiple voices and points of view into the room, and it welcomes a both/and approach to solving dilemmas and working within constraints. Finding yourself in an unfamiliar situation, a leader must adopt a learner's approach and be willing to let others who are expert lead. This requires openness that increases the creative tension and constructive disruption, managed by a leader's ability to calm emotions and make sense of complex, often confusing, situations.

Increasing diversity and inclusion during the digital transformation brings together people who don't know each other and may not have a personal relationship. Leading in these situations necessitates managing anxiety *and* complacency. Anxiety arises when people or teams are faced with challenges and the way forward is complex or unknown. Reflection is a technique that leaders can use to contain anxiety, allowing the tension to dissipate through conversation and exploration of differing ideas. When leaders encourage honest self-reflection, they can help people make sense of uncertainty and the obstacles they face. During reflection, teams and individuals are able to discuss the emotions of the situation and how their actions, their behaviors, and their interdependence impact it. Collectively they can determine how best to move forward.

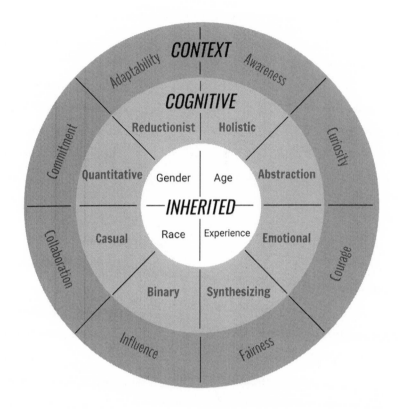

Figure 9.1. **Leading digital transformation requires two environments. Inclusivity—which creates the context in which everyone can participate and contribute—and diversity—which encourages the use of all thinking styles and multiple points of view. This model presents an approach to diversity and inclusion that is radically different compared to conventional approaches.**

Sometimes, though, anxiety is low—which seems a favorable environment. But transformational leaders know that when this is the case complacency can threaten, and these leaders must encourage exploration, courage, and disruption by providing provocative metaphors, personal stories of risk, and questions that provoke curiosity and experimentation. During times like these, leaders should facilitate and let others take the reins, leading themselves to find a way forward.

During digital transformation the focus is less on one's authority and more on one's influence. This shift in power from a person (the leader) to the transformational goal works to enable people to change their minds and behaviors.[3] Leading the charge in any given situation, context, or moment means bringing others along with you. In this sense it is a local phenomenon, one that begins by recognizing and amplifying small, local ideas that can be assembled into large, complex change. This allows the immensity of transformation in large enterprises to be chunked into bite-sized pieces that people can identify with, connect to, and handle with greater ease.

A PLAYBOOK FOR DIGITAL TRANSFORMATION

Leading in the digital environment requires new skills, knowledge, and activities. Things are happening too fast, and innovation is coming from too many places to predict and plan as you have in the past. The top of the organizational pyramid is no longer in control, and the risk of inaction is greater than the risk of a big strategic bet. Leading digital means making deep rather than superficial changes to your business and organization. The transformational journey requires leaders to understand the growth and innovation that drives the digital market ecosystem. No one gets to jump over the digital challenge and land untouched.

The organizational disruption that a digital transformation causes requires leaders to act by amplifying destabilizing forces and dampening stabilizing forces, opening the way for people to let go and jettison what is holding them back (behaviors, processes, monolithic code . . .

---

3 John Bargh, *Before You Know It: The Unconscious Reasons We Do What We Do* (New York: Touchstone, 2017).

anything). If someone in the organization sees a way forward, a solution, or a relationship that needs to be built (all destabilizing forces), amplify that; provide encouragement and reward for taking initiative. When actions or activities favor the status quo (stabilizing forces), dampen them using inquiry and probes to understand intent and illuminate alternative, more transformational ways forward. Unlocking the potential that others bring to the transformation occurs when leaders encourage social networks and experimentation, provide focused challenges even without clear solutions, and manage anxiety.

Often the journey feels like two steps forward and one step back. You need to tackle entrenched mindsets, behaviors, and reward systems, not to mention practices related to hiring, compensation, and firing. Making these your focus ensures that there will be plenty of room for those leaders around you to step up and be accountable for transforming their respective parts of the organization.

All these tools and techniques, however, don't help if you don't know where you are going. Since leading is required *across* the organization, we need a playbook we can all follow, even if we are marching to a different cadence (Figure 9.2). Think of your journey as having four phases:

- Define: Set vision and direction.
- Design: Invest in a few critical initiatives, experiments to kick off the transformation.
- Mobilize: Share learnings to build momentum throughout the company and onboard new initiatives, second generation experiments.
- Adapt: Prepare for the next wave of transformation.

Although these phases are the same for everyone, they happen only when leaders are ready to take their group, division, or

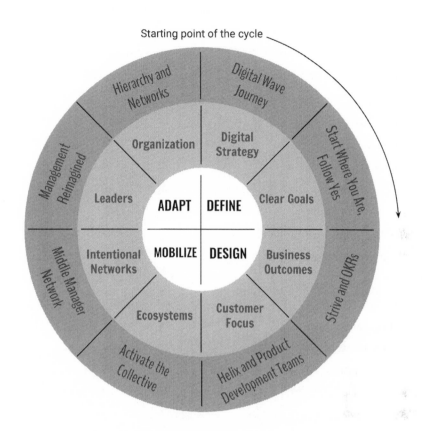

Figure 9.2. The Surge Playbook takes the company on an iterative journey through the digital waves. Every ending is also a new beginning. The faster you cycle through the journey, the faster you create value for your company and customers.

business through the journey. This means that different groups will start their journey at different times and from various starting points (initial conditions). For senior executives, the organization will seem chaotic, becoming a mosaic of products and teams all at different points in the transformation journey, encountering different obstacles and needing different kinds of support, resources, and structure. This is what makes your job interesting and challenging.

The define phase enables you to use the Digital Wave Model to explain the journey and emphasize the continuous nature of the transformation, highlighting that the organizational transformations are as important as the technical. Explore where the different parts of your company are currently operating (start where you are) and how far through the waves they need to go to remain competitive.

With this in mind, set aspirational goals for the whole company for the next 12 months. Decide which product-organizational slices you will take through the journey first, for example, an end-to-end product-based group of 150-200, using need, capability, and leadership to prioritize. Be sure to *follow yes*. Then move into the next phase, design.

Design begins your focus on the transformational cohorts you have identified, investing in them and their transformation. Invite the business to lead the transformation and start by identifying their customers and the outcomes they need to achieve to continuously create value for them. If you are shifting from project development to product development, you may have additional work to do helping everyone get out of the weeds and into a customer-focused, outside-in perspective.

Workshops to define the product and rethink the organization of the product development ecosystem are a good way to start. This allows you to establish the middle manager network and gives them a chance to integrate the business and technical backlogs as well as to create a transformational backlog. Now is also the time to introduce Helix and Strive to provide the structure needed to make the big changes you are asking for. Customer-focused approaches, such as empathy and customer journey maps, fit nicely into the Helix framework and provide complementary work for both business and technical teams. We have found that leadership and structure are often enough to replace the call for more resources in these first experiments.

With a few initiatives underway, other leaders will show up at your door, wanting to be the next to transform. You are officially in the mobilize phase. Transform by ecosystem where you can, and begin to manage the company's assets to produce synergies that generate new customer value and services. This is one of the huge benefits that enterprises have over startups.

As the collective activates and becomes mobilized, more innovative opportunities will present themselves. Be ready to scale your efforts and don't be afraid to let the whole company diverge — you will find times for convergence as you move forward. Scaling by using middle manager networks ensures that knowledge and techniques are shared across the company. Encourage people to learn from each other and not just from your transformation team.

Momentum builds and the many moving parts require adaptation to take advantage of the changes that occur. This adaptation is what turns the company from a homogeneous organization into robust, diverse, and learning ecosystems. Using both hierarchy and networks, the organization will dynamically adapt to market trends and customer needs. The emerging hierarchy-network structure (the hypertext organization) allows you to achieve this without mandating disruptive reorganization, while still being able to flex, rerole, and fully utilize every employee. Soon you will see the entire product ecosystem poised to move to the next wave and begin their transformation journey again.

Leading digital involves strategically and intentionally activating networks of people and encouraging them to transform your company. Individuals who are collectively capable of leading at a moment's notice can rise to meet the challenges of almost any situation the organization faces. Networks of middle managers help you cocreate and implement your digital vision and strategy. In these ways *Surge* allows you to generate a thousand minirevolutions that keep the whole organization at the edge of chaos without losing the transparency and alignment that staying in the sweet spot requires.

CHART YOUR COURSE RECAP

Leading digital means championing the concept of transformation in place (TIP) (Chapter 1). Find your positive deviants and nurture the 12 percent that form your tipping point network. Intentionally take them with you as you work with others so that they can learn the skills of transformation. Coach them to lead in their daily work and to engage the rest of the organization. Practice leading by interacting and engaging with them. Then step back and let them go.

Become an observer. See the adaptive and begin working *on* the organization. View the whole company as a living system. Provide opportunities to reflect so that people learn to correct course as they work. Walk around and get to know people; gather their ideas and turn them into experiments they can lead. This shifts the culture away from a focus on authority and toward a test and learn environment.

Question, hypothesize, experiment. Always search for, and focus on, the experimental question. What are we trying to understand and for the sake of what? Engage diverse stakeholders in every experiment, giving everyone a role to play that legitimizes his or her point of view. Be willing to question the organization's sacred cows and address the hidden elephants whether people want to discuss them or not.

KEY TAKEAWAYS: CHART YOUR COURSE

Executives:

As teams begin to self-manage, you, their leader, are freed up to do different work, such as working across boundaries with other parts of the company and coaching and educating positive deviants and key influencers. These new tasks give you the opportunity to practice listening, ask probing questions, and work with others to find and develop their transformational ideas.

This is a good time to focus on finding fresh ways to monitor and track the value of work being done. Many digital companies are switching from focusing on return on investment (ROI) to return on assets (ROA) as they increase their agility. Some have decided that this is the disruptive moment to move to Beyond Budgeting or radically change performance review processes. Regardless, now is the time to set the stage for rapid business innovation.

Transformation Leaders:

Guide the company toward self-organization, but don't skip the lessons needed for self-management and self-governance. Self-organization often arises based on customer needs, so encourage teams to understand and organize around the customer experience and journey. Self-organization also occurs as cross-functional groups work together to simplify outdated processes and decompose monolithic applications.

In all cases, leading involves helping others find the balance between collaboration and urgency, immediate results and longer-term outcomes, operational excellence and innovation. Leading digital requires you to act as an organizational architect, maintaining continuous transformation and inspiring people to work collectively and to care about the enterprise. This calls for your willingness to take on the challenge of people, working through others, rather than doing everything yourself.

Managers:

With the emergence of ecosystems and platforms, your focus shifts to ensuring good self-governance practices. Help emerging ecosystems write charters to tackle complex systemic problems or deliver novel products and services. Use self-governance to oscillate between hierarchy and networks. Make processes, such as change and program management, calibrated, not rigid and heavy-handed. As self-management and self-governance increase, be on the lookout for cognitive bias and conditions that dampen diversity. Tackle these as leftover behavioral problems , and coach people to embrace diversity and inclusion.

Employees:

Construct your own networks of exchange and information transfer. Begin experimenting and using the diverge-converge cycle in your daily work. Stay positive and constructive, reflecting on the system and culture you have established with the intent to evolve it to better serve you. Set up meetings for ideation and innovation rather than status reporting. Support each other, and lead when someone is having an off day or feeling overwhelmed. Encourage information sharing so that the "crowd" has enough information to make good decisions.

A lot had happened in one year . . . for all four of them. Ethan had been poached by a large, global enterprise to lead their newly initiated digital transformation. Gina was promoted and asked to take on a global strategy role to amplify and make the most of all the company's digital commercial platforms. Anna's global entertainment company acquired a midsized competitor, and she was called upon to lead the integration of both technology and business. And Abe had his hands full with a successful technical transformation that was now integrating with businesses across the firm.

After catching up on their busy work lives, the conversation comes around to the difference a year has made to each of them personally.

"I honestly never thought I'd leave technology," Gina says. "I am a geek. And once a geek, I thought, always a geek. But I'm finding that everyone is a geek in their own niche."

"I'm not a geek," Ethan blurts out. "I feel like Abe did a year ago. I was a big fish in a small pond, and now I'm in a huge pond and not even sure I'm a fish. What was I thinking?"

"I feel like you," Anna says, her face bright and her voice buoyant. "I am eating the dog food we dished out to Abe last year . . . and some days it takes a strong drink to wash it down. Abe, please tell me that we were right on all accounts!"

"You were . . ." Abe answers, hesitantly.

"Uh-oh," Ethan verbalizes what their faces portray.

Abe smiles. "No, you were right. Still, looking back, I don't think I fully appreciated until just this moment how much I had to change. You warned me, at least I think you did; and I think I knew it, but I had no idea how to change or what I personally had to 'change into.' So it's my turn to ask you all: How or what do you need to *change into* to meet the challenges and opportunities of your new roles? Because, you know, I suppose it's possible that I may be following in your footsteps in the near future!"

Silence.

Abe continues, "I have another observation that I am just beginning to appreciate, and that is just how much and how critical a role organizational culture plays in transformation. At least it is for us."

Another thoughtful pause.

"Well, let me respond by saying we've created a transformation guru," Anna chides. "In all honestly, I feel like I am reinventing myself, and, truthfully, I'm loving it. It is interesting that you bring up the culture piece, Abe, because I'm now faced with two completely different cultures. Integrating the technology is the easiest part; it's something I can hand over to others. But integrating the business and culture is different. I have lots of folks who want to tell me what to do from a business perspective—*and* how to do it. I am trying to figure out who has the customer at heart versus having their own agenda. No one, and I mean no one, is talking about integrating the culture, building new relationships, and establishing human networks between the two companies that can, and will, get all that other stuff done."

"I definitely agree on the culture piece, and I haven't even changed companies," Gina says building on Anna's comments. "I'm not sure I have to reinvent myself, but stay tuned on that. I am finding that I have to use interpersonal skills that I can't recall using since I was a teenager . . . which is occasionally awkward but somehow very freeing."

Ethan rolls his eyes. "Gina, you are one of the most socially savvy people I know. You are an intellectual powerhouse who makes everyone around you feel as if they are rock stars. Now me, I feel like I am on a first date with everyone I meet these days. And, boy, do I *feel* the hidden agendas and power plays even if I don't know where they originate or why! They all want to know what I think so they can figure out how to work around me. So I've had to discover that hearing everyone else's ideas first is the safest way to protect my 'transformation boy-wonder' image *and* avoid the political quicksand at the same time. And culture," Ethan turns to Abe, "you are spot-on. The fact that I am outside the corporate culture is a blessing and a curse."

"Ha! You're a virus," Abe jokes, "working hard to infect the host and spread new ideas to all parts of the company—all in a good way, of course." Abe pauses, thinks, then laughs, "Gee, look what we've turned into. Anna is reinventing herself, Gina is a teenager again, Ethan is a virus . . . and I'm . . . " he searches for the right word, "well, I'm a tightrope walker."

"Now that is not what I thought you would say!" Anna says.

Ethan and Gina laugh.

"Yeah, Abe. That requires some explanation."

"Well, I feel that I'm up on a tightrope, and I know I shouldn't look down . . . or I'll lose my balance." Abe says. "But the closer I think I am to the end, the farther the rope stretches out into the distance. The other side always seems just about within reach until . . . it isn't! And the temptation to look down gets greater and greater."

Ethan pounds the table laughing heartily in agreement. "That is the perfect description. I feel exactly that way myself. Just when I think I have the greatest insight that will untangle the hairball . . . I don't. But, and this is the funny *and* wonderful thing: I keep making progress. The stuff we talked about last year, it works. I am pouring new content into the frameworks, and they continue producing the outcomes I need when and where I need them."

"'Trust the process!'" Abe chimes in. "That's what you told me.

You've got to turn people loose and let them run. Be clear about what you're asking for, and when you see that spark, let them take the lead. Hold them accountable, for sure, but let them take you and the organization to places not yet seen, or even imagined."

"That's it, Abe," Gina claps her hands together, her eyes wide. "It's trust. That is the answer to everything. Trust the process. Trust yourself. Remember at the beginning you trusted *us* rather than the process or yourself?"

"That's right!" Anna says eagerly. "That is the human part we so often forget in our desire to create the perfect strategy and execute the most powerful tactics. You've suddenly made me realize that I have been so busy doing things that I've forgotten that the first thing I need to do is get people who don't know each other to *trust* each other."

Ethan furrows his brow, thinking out loud. "It's that cultural thing again. People all over the company need to trust each other in order to deliver, to share information and resources, to stop the power plays and hidden agendas. Then everyone can begin to work for the customer wholeheartedly." Suddenly, Ethan's face lights up. "Discovery time for me too: That's what I need to do now. Get people working *for* the customer instead of *against* each other."

"And now that you mention it," Abe jumps in, "when you trust each other to work together, and trust the customer to know what they actually want, you can stop guessing and start really creating value."

"There you have it," Gina laughs, "we have organizational peace and prosperity. And on that note . . . anyone having dessert?"

"Thought you'd never ask." Ethan grabs the menu. "Who wants apple pie?"

"With vanilla ice cream?" Gina asks.

"Absolutely," Abe agrees, waving at the waiter.

"Successful employee-engagement practice is not about plugging in a set of tools and techniques that you just read about in some hotshot guru's latest book—and then expecting engaged employees to magically appear."

—Richard H. Axelrod, "All Aboard? Why Companies Still Don't Get Employee Engagement Right."

FOLLOW YES!

A few years ago we had the opportunity to work with the division of a large media company that was in the midst of an agile transformation that had stalled. Several previous starts had never gained enough traction to take hold across the company, despite a strong focus on the introduction of new agile methods and tools. Working with the executive in charge and his senior leadership team (SLT), we restarted their journey with a different set of assumptions about how and why they were struggling.

Instead of focusing on methods and tools, we focused on people and leadership. We engaged their middle managers and leaders in a series of experiential adaptive leadership workshops. We even invited the SLT to attend as observers, which many did, creating remarkable transparency. Each session started the same, then diverged as each group of managers and leaders initiated critical conversations with each other that defined the experience and workshop outcomes.

After nearly every workshop, a few people approached us wanting to do more, to dive deeper, try out ideas that came up in the workshop, or address specific challenges they faced using the methods in the exercises. In each case we encouraged their ideas, picking up on their lead . . . following yes.

Following the workshop, we supported these leaders in ways that gave them the space and means to explore technical and organizational solutions to their challenges and opportunities. These workshops unleashed actions and exploration across the division. In less than two months participants had initiated six very different transformational ideas, which a year later radically transformed the entire organization! This outcome was not some magic trick or miracle, but the natural outcome of leaders, managers, and teams choosing to think and act as positive deviants, jettisoning a certain "victim" attitude and increasingly adopting a growth mindset.

The result was unprecedented creativity and breakthrough performance despite facing many of the restrictions and obstacles they previously blamed for their lack of success. How and why this happened is simple: People had discovered a reservoir of possibilities and energy that was formerly untapped and unused. Right now this seemingly unavailable human capacity to achieve remarkable things exists in *your* company. But we acknowledge that discovering and unleashing this potential for transformative change can seem unimaginable. This is largely because success in this type of endeavor does not use the old methods of technical adoption or corporate restructuring. Success is instead a journey of personal and organizational transformation—and the digital disruption is just what you need to get started!

While the digital tsunami has brought unprecedented volatility and complexity (indeed all the elements of VUCA) to traditional enterprises, *Surge* reveals new ways to embrace these dynamics to enable your organization to achieve and innovate as never before. We have shown how you can use disruption to your advantage, developing ways to navigate through uncharted territory. The strategic use of uncertainty paired with human potential is the prevailing principle and purpose of transformation.

To get started, let's take a moment to reflect on the assets you already have in your company, all the resources you need to begin the digital wave journey and to successfully navigate to Wave 3 and beyond. Ask yourself: "What is it about our company, right this moment, that I am excited and optimistic about?" What actions can you take to realize the opportunity that that represents? And what personal strengths do you have that enable you to achieve the outcomes you desire?

Your answers to these questions are your initial *yeses!* Follow them! Find out how you can initiate the transformation they represent—right now. And simply proceed—actively, intentionally, openly—one step after another, and then another . . . .

TRANSFORMATION IS PERSONAL

One of the more rewarding outcomes we regularly see by those employing the concepts and tools of *Surge* is not just the corporate renewal that occurs, but the personal transformations. As you integrate the elements of continuous transformation into your organizational life and your daily practice at work, you will find that these also influence those around you; they are contagious. The more you practice curiosity, for example, the more curiosity takes root in the actions and behaviors of others. As you practice leading, drawing upon those personal experiences that directly inspire you, your stories and actions will provide memes that encourage others to lead. And the more others change, the more you transform as well . . . creating a virtuous cycle.

As you practice following yes you learn to let go, to jettison the things that hold you back, to maintain your forward motion. Even those things that once nourished you—your title, skills, or achievements—may slow you down or unbalance you. Let them go, even when you are reluctant to leave them behind. They are gratifying, they are comforting . . . but they can keep you stuck, making you vulnerable during change. Be vigilant and avoid letting things like these prevent you from acting in new ways, trying new things, or thinking differently.

As we've discussed throughout, you are creating a company that encourages ongoing experimentation, which means you must continuously experiment and work *on* yourself too. Of course it is awkward to be a learner, you may not get it right the first time—no one does! Learn to design personal experiments that allow you to stretch, reach, and explore. Your *company's* future *depends* on finding ways to promote the practice and culture of safe-to-fail experimentation and learning, and you can lead the way. At every step of the digital wave journey, you should be using phrases like, "What if we were to . . .?"; "I've been thinking about it, and maybe we could try . . ."; "Well, that didn't work—so what were our hypotheses and assumptions?"; and "I think I know why it didn't work, so this time let's try . . .". And hearing these kinds of comments made by others is a good indicator that the cycle of thinking, experimenting, and learning is taking hold. In short, the company is transforming.

Finally, recall our mantra that all organizations already have the solutions to their struggles embedded within them. You aren't broken. You simply need to find ways to adapt to market challenges and address customer needs. There are a million things we can tell you (and we've told you many of them already), but you have the optimal vantage point: Understanding where you are, following yes, and embracing the journey of transformation. Along the way, you can review the things we've discussed and apply them to the challenge or opportunity you're facing. Let our words function as not only a guide, but also as encouragement, especially in those moments when you and those around you feel the most challenged.

PARTING WORDS ON TRANSFORMATION

It's a fact of today's business world that unless you embrace digital transformation, you are going nowhere. The excellent news is that digital transformation not only *allows,* but even *requires,* everything you can imagine and anything you can do. In choosing the journey of continuous transformation, you ensure that no idea is wasted and no experiment is without value. You actually have at your disposal all you need to overcome whatever challenge presents itself.

Digital transformation will result in outcomes you can't possibly imagine now because you will create them as you go — by *the act* of reinventing yourself and your company. No matter what yes you follow first, you are now equipped to navigate your way through the digital tsunami. All you need to do is set sail!

APPENDIX

Actions That Anyone Can Take for Each Chapter in Section II

For those interested in learning more, visit www.surgetoolkit.com for in-depth exploration of these ideas.

Social Memes — Activate the Collective:

- Listen to your internal dialogue as well as the conversations going on inside your company. How are you contributing to these stories? Ask others for feedback.

- Pay attention to the words you're using and hearing within various business units, inside functional departments, and under different leaders. Notice those that are distinctly positive or negative, confusing or clear. Provide feedback to improve the corporate narrative.

- Find conversations that reveal vulnerabilities and frustration, particularly in relation to adaptation and change; understand and address these very human emotions. Remove these barriers to change and help people stay motivated.

- Consider the story that your company is telling your ecosystem of customers and partners. How does this affect the transformational work you need to do and your ability to work with them?

- Identify communities that contribute social cohesion and the positive deviants that are driving change — enlist them as transformational leaders to write and spread the digital transformation story.

- Share your own personal story about your life in the company — where you've been, where you are, and where you're headed.

Helix Cycles — Operationalize Continuous Transformation:

- Understand who your customer is and define your customer's needs as precisely as possible.

- Perform adaptive and technical work in a synergistic manner rather than separately. Make your participation meaningful to yourself and others.

- Learn how to write hypotheses and test them using well designed experiments. Exploration, learning, experimentation, and change aren't initiatives — they are the responsibility of every employee.

- Perfect your ability to see what needs to be done organizationally (on) to achieve your business goals (in). Stay close to the flow of ideas and use immersive, experiential techniques (versus PowerPoint).

- Act before you have all the answers and avoid inaction at all costs.

- Be relentlessly customer focused; build products and services for them, not you. Understand and use new data and analytics.

Strive Framework — Advance Breakthrough Performance:

- Make sure you understand the corporate strategy and goals. If you don't, ask.

- Structure your daily work as OKRs: Write objectives and key results that you are working to achieve this quarter.

- Write three levels of achievement for each of your KRs: a moonshot (1.0), an awesome result (0.7), and a doable stretch output (0.3).

- For your 1.0 and 0.7 levels find and enroll horizontal partners that can contribute to your success.

- Even if you are not using Strive you can have your own, personal weekly huddle. Answer the questions to track your progress and make forecasts that you can share with others.

- Become a contributor. Find something that you are interested in but not involved in, and get involved.

Intentional Networks — Engage the Middle:

- Give the middle network the role of operationalizing your digital transformation strategy.
- Use local middle networks to coordinate the tactical and operational aspects of execution, linking the organization horizontally.
- Make it the job of middle managers to flow information up, down, and across the company, not hoard it.
- Recognize and use the knowledge that lives in the network to access all the skills and capabilities of the company.
- Promote different points of view, cognitive diversity, and establish the conditions under which diversity flourishes.
- Become an information broker and a boundary spanner.

Leading Digital — Chart Your Course:

- Begin by embarking upon your own personal leadership journey. Find a new way of doing something you do daily.
- Remind yourself that your view of the organization, business, opportunity, or problem contains your personal cognitive biases — then seek the input of people who are not like you.
- Identify your personal limitations but amplify your strengths (strut your stuff). Have the courage to make bets others won't.
- Enroll rather than control; enjoy the daily adventure.
- Ask hard questions. Amplify and dampen behaviors, actions, and events to correct course.
- Learn improv and use it to challenge established norms, conventions, and traditions.

INDEX

Made in the USA
Middletown, DE
06 November 2018